Latin-English Sunday Missal

The Ordinary of the 1962 Typical Edition

Latin-English Sunday Missal

The Ordinary of the 1962 Typical Edition

Roman Catholic Books

P.O. Box 2286 • Fort Collins, CO 80522

BooksforCatholics.com

Cover Photo: Scala/Art Resource, NY

ISBN 978-1-929291-92-2

Printed in the U.S.A.

Contents

Publisher's Preface

On May 16, 2007, Cardinal Dario Castrillon Hoyos, President of the Pontifical Ecclesia Dei Commission, which was established by Pope John Paul II in 1988 to encourage wider use of the traditional Latin Missal, delivered a speech on behalf of Pope Benedict XVI in which he explained the Holy Father's new and greater planned expansion of the same Missal.

Cardinal Hoyos said in part:

"The Holy Father has the intention of extending to the entire Latin Church the possibility of celebrating Holy Mass and the Sacraments according to the liturgical books promulgated by Blessed John XXIII in 1962. There is today a new and renewed interest for this liturgy, which has never been abolished and which, as we have said, is considered a treasure....The Holy Father believes that the time has come to ease, as the first Cardinalatial Commission of 1986 had wished to do, the access to this liturgy, making it an extraordinary form of the one Roman Rite.

"It is...a generous offer of the Vicar of Christ who, as an expression of his pastoral will, wishes to put at the disposal of the whole Church all the treasures of the Latin Liturgy which for centuries has nourished the spiritual life of so many generations of Catholic faithful. The Holy Father wishes to preserve the immense spiritual, cultural, and aesthetic treasures linked to the Ancient Liturgy. The revival of this wealth is linked to the no less precious one of the current Liturgy of the Church."

In this spirit, Roman Catholic Books offers this Sunday Latin Mass Booklet Missal using the ordinary of 1962 typical edition.

We pray that it may further the unity of the Church and the growth in charity of all who pray with it.

Events from the Life of Moses
Botticelli

Tridentine Mass

1962 Typical Edition

THE ASPERGES

ASPERGES ME, Domine, hyssopo, et mundabor: lavabis me, et super nivem dealbabor.

MISERERE MEI, Deus, secundum magnam misericordiam tuam.

P. Gloria Patri, et Filio, et Spiritui Sancto.

S. Sicut erat in principio, et nunc, et semper,
et in sæcula sæculorum. Amen.

ASPERGES ME, Domine, hyssopo, et mundabor: lavabis me, et super nivem dealbabor.

P. Ostende nobis, Domine, misericordiam tuam.
S. Et salutare tuum da nobis.
P. Domine, exaudi orationem meam.
S. Et clamor meus ad te veniat.
P. Dominus vobiscum.
S. Et cum spiritu tuo.
P. Oremus.

EXAUDI NOS, Domine sancte, Pater omnipotens, æterne Deus, et mittere digneris sanctum Angelum tuum de cælis, qui custodiat, foveat, protegat, visitet, atque defendat omnes habitantes in hoc habitaculo. Per Christum Dominum nostrum.
S. Amen.

VIDI AQUAM egredientem de templo, a latere dextro, alleluia: et omnes ad quos pervenit aqua ista salvi facti sunt, et dicent, alleluia, alleluia.

CONFITEMINI DOMINO, quoniam bonus: quoniam in sæculum misericordia ejus.

THE ASPERGES

STAND

THOU SHALT SPRINKLE ME, O Lord, with hyssop, and I shall be cleansed; Thou shalt wash me, and I shall become whiter than snow.
HAVE MERCY ON ME, O God, according to Thy great mercy.

P. Glory be to the Father, and to the Son,
and to the Holy Ghost.
S. As it was in the beginning, is now, and
ever shall be, world without end. Amen.

THOU SHALT SPRINKLE ME, O Lord, with hyssop, and I shall be cleansed; Thou shalt wash me, and I shall become whiter than snow.
P. Show us, O Lord, Thy mercy.
S. And grant us Thy salvation.
P. O Lord, hear my prayer.
S. And let my cry come unto Thee.
P. The Lord be with you.
S. And with thy spirit.
P. Let us pray.

HEAR US, O holy Lord, Almighty Father, everlasting God, and vouchsafe to send Thy holy Angel from heaven, to guard, cherish, protect, visit and defend all that are assembled in this place: Through Christ our Lord.
S. Amen.

I SAW WATER flowing from the right side of the temple, alleluia; and all they to whom that water came were saved, and they shall say, alleluia, alleluia.

PRAISE THE LORD, for He is good; for His mercy endureth forever.

SIT

Crucifixion with attendant Saints Fra Angelico

Transfiguration
Fra Angelico

ORDO MISSÆ

MASS OF THE CATECHUMENS

IN NOMINE PATRIS, ✠ et Filii, et Spiritus Sancti. Amen.

P. Introibo ad altare Dei.
S. Ad Deum qui lætificat juventutem meam.

Judica Me—Psalm 42

JUDICA ME, Deus, et discerne causam meam de gente non sancta: ab homine iniquo, et doloso erue me.

S. Quia tu es, Deus, fortitudo mea: / quare me repulisti, / et quare tristis incedo, / dum affligit me inimicus?
P. Emitte lucem tuam, et veritatem tuam: ipsa me deduxerunt, et adduxerunt in montem sanctum tuum, et in tabernacula tua.
S. Et introibo ad altare Dei: / ad Deum qui lætificat juventutem meam.
P. Confitebor tibi in cithara, Deus, Deus meus: quare tristis es, anima mea, et quare conturbas me?
S. Spera in Deo, / quoniam adhuc confitebor illi: salutare vultus mei, / et Deus meus.
P. Gloria Patri, et Filio, et Spiritui Sancto.

S. Sicut erat in principio et nunc, et semper, / et in sæcula sæculorum. Amen.

THE ORDINARY OF THE MASS

KNEEL

MASS OF THE CATECHUMENS

IN THE NAME OF THE FATHER, ✠ and of the Son, and of the Holy Ghost. Amen.

Priest: I will go in unto the Altar of God.
Server: To God, Who giveth joy to my youth.

Psalm 42—Judica Me

JUDGE ME, O God, and distinguish my cause from the nation that is not holy: deliver me from the unjust and deceitful man.

S. For Thou, O God, art my strength: why hast Thou cast me off? and why do I go sorrowful whilst the enemy afflicteth me?
P. Send forth Thy light and Thy truth: they have led me and brought me unto Thy holy hill, and into Thy tabernacles.
S. And I will go in unto the Altar of God: unto God, Who giveth joy to my youth.
P. I will praise Thee upon the harp, O God, my God: why art thou sad, O my soul? and why dost thou disquiet me?
S. Hope thou in God, for I will yet praise Him: Who is the salvation of my countenance, and my God.
P. Glory be to the Father, and to the Son, and to the Holy Ghost.
S. As it was in the beginning, is now, and ever shall be, world without end. Amen.

P. Introibo ad altare Dei.
S. Ad Deum qui lætificat juventutem meam.

P. Adjutorium nostrum ✠ in nomine Domini.
S. Qui fecit cælum et terram.

P. Confiteor Deo omnipotenti, etc. (as below)
S. Misereatur tui omnipotens Deus, / et dimissis peccatis tuis, / perducat te ad vitam æternam.
P. Amen.

CONFITEOR DEO OMNIPOTENTI, / beatæ Mariæ semper Virgini, / beato Michaeli Archangelo, / beato Joanni Baptistæ, / sanctis Apostolis Petro et Paulo, / omnibus Sanctis, et tibi, Pater: / quia peccavi nimis cogitatione, verbo et opere: / mea culpa, mea culpa, mea maxima culpa. / Ideo precor beatam Mariam semper Virginem, / beatum Michaelem Archangelum, / beatum Joannem Baptistam, / sanctos Apostolos Petrum et Paulum, / omnes Sanctos, et te, Pater, / orare pro me ad Dominum Deum nostrum.

P. Misereatur vestri omnipotens Deus, et dimissis peccatis vestris, perducat vos ad vitam æternam.
S. Amen.
P. Indulgentiam, ✠ absolutionem, et remissionem peccatorum nostrorum tribuat nobis omnipotens et misericors Dominus.
S. Amen.

P. Deus, tu conversus vivificabis nos.
S. Et plebs tua lætabitur in te.
P. Ostende nobis, Domine, misericordiam tuam.
S. Et salutare tuum da nobis.
P. Domine, exaudi orationem meam.
S. Et clamor meus ad te veniat.
P. Dominus vobiscum.
S. Et cum spiritu tuo.

P. I will go in unto the Altar of God.
S. Unto God, Who giveth joy to my youth.

P. Our help ✠ is in the Name of the Lord.
S. Who hath made heaven and earth.

P. I confess to Almighty God, etc. (as below)
S. May Almighty God have mercy upon you, forgive you your sins, and bring you to life everlasting.
P. Amen.

I CONFESS TO ALMIGHTY GOD, to blessed Mary ever Virgin, to blessed Michael the Archangel, to blessed John the Baptist, to the holy Apostles Peter and Paul, to all the Saints, and to you, Father, that I have sinned exceedingly, in thought, word and deed: through my fault, through my fault, through my most grievous fault. Therefore I beseech blessed Mary ever Virgin, blessed Michael the Archangel, blessed John the Baptist, the holy Apostles Peter and Paul, all the Saints, and you, Father, to pray to the Lord our God for me.

P. May Almighty God have mercy upon you, forgive you your sins, and bring you to life everlasting.
S. Amen.
P. May the Almighty and merciful God grant us pardon, ✠ absolution, and remission of our sins.
S. Amen.

P. Thou wilt turn, O God, and bring us to life.
S. And Thy people shall rejoice in Thee.
P. Show us, O Lord, Thy mercy.
S. And grant us Thy salvation.
P. O Lord, hear my prayer.
S. And let my cry come unto Thee.
P. The Lord be with you.
S. And with thy spirit.

P. Oremus.

AUFER a nobis, quæsumus, Domine, iniquitates nostras: ut ad Sancta sanctorum puris mereamur mentibus introire. Per Christum Dominum nostrum. Amen.

ORAMUS TE, Domine, per merita Sanctorum tuorum, quorum reliquiæ hic sunt, et omnium Sanctorum: ut indulgere digneris omnia peccata mea. Amen.

THE INTROIT Tobias 12:6

Benedicta sit sancta Trinitas, atque indivisa unitas: confitebimur ei, quia fecit nobiscum misericordiam suam. Domine Dominus noster, quam admirabile est nomen tuum in universa terra!

Gloria Patri, et Filio, et Spiritui Sancto. Sicut erat in principio, et nunc, et semper: et in sæcula sæculorum. Amen.

Benedicta sit sancta Trinitas, atque indivisa unitas: confitebimur ei, quia fecit nobiscum misericordiam suam.

P. KYRIE, eleison.
S. Kyrie, eleison.
P. Kyrie, eleison.
S. Christe, eleison.
P. Christe, eleison.
S. Christe, eleison.
P. Kyrie, eleison.
S. Kyrie, eleison.
P. Kyrie, eleison.

P. Let us pray.

The Priest Ascends the Altar

TAKE AWAY from us our iniquities, we entreat Thee, O Lord, that with pure minds we may worthily enter into the Holy of Holies. Through Christ our Lord. Amen.

WE BESEECH THEE, O Lord, by the merits of Thy Saints, whose relics are here, and of all the Saints, that Thou wilt deign to pardon me all my sins. Amen.

THE INTROIT (Proper)

Blessed be the holy Trinity, and undivided Unity: we will give glory to Him because He hath shown His mercy to us. O Lord, our Lord, how admirable is Thy Name in all the earth.

Glory be to the Father, and to the Son, and to the Holy Ghost. As it was in the beginning, is now, and ever shall be, world without end. Amen.

Blessed be the holy Trinity and undivided Unity: we will give glory to Him because He hath shown His mercy to us.

Kyrie Eleison

P. LORD, have mercy on us.
S. Lord, have mercy on us.
P. Lord, have mercy on us.
S. Christ, have mercy on us.
P. Christ, have mercy on us.
S. Christ, have mercy on us.
P. Lord, have mercy on us.
S. Lord, have mercy on us.
P. Lord, have mercy on us.

Gloria in excelsis Deo, / et in terra pax hominibus / bonæ voluntatis. / Laudamus te. / Benedicimus te. / Adoramus te. / Glorificamus te. / Gratias agimus tibi / propter magnam gloriam tuam. / Domine Deus, / Rex cælestis, / Deus Pater omnipotens. / Domine Fili unigenite, / Jesu Christe. / Domine Deus, / Agnus Dei, / Filius Patris. / Qui tollis peccata mundi, / miserere nobis. / Qui tollis peccata mundi, / suscipe deprecationem nostram. / Qui sedes ad dexteram Patris, / miserere nobis. / Quoniam tu solus Sanctus. / Tu solus Dominus. / Tu solus Altissimus, Jesu Christe. / Cum Sancto Spiritu, ✠ / in gloria Dei Patris. / Amen.

P. Dominus vobiscum.
S. Et cum spiritu tuo.
P. Oremus.

THE COLLECT(S)

Omnipotens sempiterne Deus, qui dedisti famulis tuis in confessione veræ fidei, æternæ Trinitatis gloriam agnoscere, et in potentia majestatis adorare unitatem: quæsumus; ut ejusdem fidei firmitate, ab omnibus semper muniamur adversis. Per Dominum nostrum Jesum Christum, Filium tuum, qui tecum vivit et regnat, in unitate Spiritus Sancti, Deus, per omnia sæcula sæculorum.
S. Amen.

THE EPISTLE Romans 11:33-36

O altitudo divitiarum sapientiæ et scientiæ Dei: quam incomprehensibilia sunt judicia ejus, et investigabiles viæ ejus! Quis enim cognovit sensum Domini? Aut quis consiliarius ejus fuit? Aut quis prior dedit illi, et retribuetur ei? Quoniam ex ipso, et per ipsum, et in ipso sunt omnia: ipsi gloria in sæcula. Amen.

S. Deo gratias.

STAND
High Mass

Gloria in Excelsis

GLORY BE TO GOD ON HIGH. And on earth peace to men of good will. We praise Thee. We bless Thee. We adore Thee. We glorify Thee. We give Thee thanks for Thy great glory. Lord God, heavenly King, God the Father Almighty. Lord Jesus Christ, Only-begotten Son, Lord God, Lamb of God, Son of the Father. Thou Who takest away the sins of the world, have mercy on us. Thou Who takest away the sins of the world, receive our prayer. Thou Who sittest at the right hand of the Father, have mercy on us. For Thou alone art holy. Thou alone art the Lord. Thou alone, O Jesus Christ, art most high. With the Holy Ghost, ✠ in the glory of God the Father. Amen.

P. The Lord be with you.
S. And with thy spirit.
P. Let us pray.

THE COLLECT(S) (Proper)

O Almighty and Everlasting God, by Whose gift Thy servants, in confessing the true Faith, acknowledge the glory of the Eternal Trinity, and adore the Unity in the power of Thy Majesty: grant that by steadfastness in the same Faith we may evermore be defended from all adversities. Through our Lord Jesus Christ Thy Son, Who liveth and reigneth with Thee in the unity of the Holy Ghost, God for ever and ever.
S. Amen.

SIT
High Mass

THE EPISTLE (Proper)

O the depth of the riches of the wisdom and of the knowledge of God! How incomprehensible are His judgments and how unsearchable His ways! For who hath known the mind of the Lord? Or who hath been His counsellor? Or who hath first given unto Him, and recompense shall be made him? For of Him, and by Him, and in Him, are all things: to Him be glory forever. Amen.

S. Thanks be to God.

THE GRADUAL

Benedictus es, Domine, qui intueris abyssos, et sedes super Cherubim. Benedictus es, Domine, in firmamento cæli, et laudabilis in sæcula.

Alleluia, alleluia. Benedictus es, Domine, Deus patrum nostrorum, et laudabilis in sæcula. Alleluia.

MUNDA COR MEUM ac labia mea, omnipotens Deus, qui labia Isaiæ Prophetæ calculo mundasti ignito: ita me tua grata miseratione dignare mundare, ut sanctum Evangelium tuum digne valeam nuntiare. Per Christum Dominum nostrum. Amen.

Jube, Domine, benedicere.

Dominus sit in corde meo, et in labiis meis: ut digne et competenter annuntiem Evangelium suum. Amen.

THE GOSPEL Matthew 28:18-20

P. Dominus vobiscum.
S. Et cum spiritu tuo.
P. ✠ Sequentia sancti Evangelii secundum Matthæum.
S. Gloria tibi, Domine.

In illo tempore: Dixit Jesus discipulis suis: Data est mihi omnis potestas in cælo, et in terra. Euntes ergo docete omnes gentes, baptizantes eos in nomine Patris, et Filii, et Spiritus Sancti: docentes eos servare omnia quæcumque mandavi vobis. Et ecce, ego vobiscum sum omnibus diebus usque ad consummationem sæculi.

S. Laus tibi, Christe.
P. Per evangelica dicta, deleantur nostra delicta.

THE GRADUAL (Proper)

Blessed art Thou, O Lord, that beholdest the depths and sittest above the Cherubim. Blessed art Thou, O Lord, in the firmament of heaven, and worthy of praise for ever.

Alleluia, alleluia. Blessed art Thou, O Lord, the God of our fathers, and worthy to be praised for ever. Alleluia.

Munda Cor Meum

CLEANSE MY HEART and my lips, O Almighty God, Who didst cleanse the lips of the prophet Isaias with a burning coal; through Thy gracious mercy so purify me that I may worthily proclaim Thy holy Gospel. Through Christ our Lord. Amen.

Grant, O Lord, Thy blessing.

May the Lord be in my heart and on my lips that I may worthily and fittingly proclaim His Gospel. Amen.

THE GOSPEL (Proper)

STAND

P. The Lord be with you.
S. And with thy spirit.
P. ✠ The continuation of the holy Gospel according to St. Matthew.
S. Glory be to Thee, O Lord.

At that time, Jesus said to His disciples: All power in heaven and on earth has been given to Me. Go, therefore, and make disciples of all nations, baptizing them in the Name of the Father, and of the Son, and of the Holy Ghost, teaching them to observe all that I have commanded you; and behold, I am with you all days even unto the consummation of the world.

S. Praise be to Thee, O Christ.
P. By the words of the Gospel may our sins be blotted out.

Sermon

SIT

Noli Me Tangere
Fra Angelico

Linaiuoli Tabernacle: Saints Peter and Mark
Fra Angelico

Credo in unum Deum, / Patrem omnipotentem, / factorem cæli et terræ, / visibilium omnium et invisibilium. / Et in unum Dominum Jesum Christum, / Filium Dei unigenitum. / Et ex Patre natum / ante omnia sæcula. / Deum de Deo, / lumen de lumine, / Deum verum de Deo vero. / Genitum, non factum, / consubstantialem Patri: / per quem omnia facta sunt. / Qui propter nos homines / et propter nostram salutem / descendit de cælis. / (here all kneel)

ET INCARNATUS EST DE SPIRITU SANCTO / EX MARIA VIRGINE: / ET HOMO FACTUS EST. (rise)

Crucifixus etiam pro nobis: / sub Pontio Pilato / passus, et sepultus est. / Et resurrexit tertia die, / secundum Scripturas. / Et ascendit in cælum: / sedet ad dexteram Patris. / Et iterum venturus est cum gloria / judicare vivos et mortuos: / cujus regni non erit finis. /

Et in Spiritum Sanctum, / Dominum et vivificantem: / qui ex Patre, Filioque procedit. / Qui cum Patre, et Filio / simul adoratur, / et conglorificatur: / qui locutus est per Prophetas./ Et unam, sanctam, catholicam / et apostolicam Ecclesiam. / Confiteor unum baptisma / in remissionem peccatorum. / Et expecto resurrectionem mortuorum. / Et vitam ✠ venturi sæculi. / Amen.

P. Dominus vobiscum.
S. Et cum spiritu tuo.
P. Oremus.

Nicene Creed

STAND

I BELIEVE IN ONE GOD, the Father Almighty, Maker of heaven and earth, and of all things visible and invisible. And in one Lord Jesus Christ, the Only-begotten Son of God. Born of the Father before all ages. God of God, Light of Light, true God of true God. Begotten, not made: consubstantial with the Father; by Whom all things were made. Who for us men, and for our salvation, came down from heaven.
(here all kneel)

AND WAS INCARNATE BY THE HOLY GHOST OF THE VIRGIN MARY: AND WAS MADE MAN. (rise)

GENUFLECT

He was crucified also for us, suffered under Pontius Pilate, and was buried. And on the third day He rose again according to the Scriptures. And He ascended into heaven, and sitteth at the right hand of the Father. And He shall come again with glory to judge the living and the dead: of Whose kingdom there shall be no end.

And in the Holy Ghost, the Lord and Giver of Life: Who proceedeth from the Father and the Son. Who together with the Father and the Son is adored and glorified: Who spoke through the Prophets. And in One, Holy, Catholic and Apostolic Church. I confess one Baptism for the remission of sins. And I look for the resurrection of the dead, and the life ✠ of the world to come. Amen.

P. The Lord be with you.
S. And with thy spirit.
P. Let us pray.

STAND

MASS OF THE FAITHFUL
Offertory

THE OFFERTORY

Benedictus sit Deus Pater, unigenitusque Dei Filius, Sanctus quoque Spiritus: quia fecit nobiscum misericordiam suam.

SUSCIPE, SANCTE PATER, omnipotens æterne Deus, hanc immaculatam hostiam, quam ego indignus famulus tuus offero tibi Deo meo vivo et vero, pro innumerabilibus peccatis, et offensionibus, et negligentiis meis, et pro omnibus circumstantibus, sed et pro omnibus fidelibus christianis vivis atque defunctis: ut mihi et illis proficiat ad salutem in vitam æternam. Amen.

DEUS, ✠ qui humanæ substantiæ dignitatem mirabiliter condidisti et mirabilius reformasti: da nobis, per hujus aquæ et vini mysterium, ejus divinitatis esse consortes, qui humanitatis nostræ fieri dignatus est particeps, Jesus Christus, Filius tuus, Dominus noster: Qui tecum vivit et regnat in unitate Spiritus Sancti, Deus: per omnia sæcula sæculorum. Amen.

MASS OF THE FAITHFUL
Offertory

THE OFFERTORY (Proper) SIT

Blessed be God, the Father, and the Only-begotten Son of God, and also the Holy Spirit: because He hath shown His mercy toward us.

Offering of the Bread and Wine

ACCEPT, O HOLY FATHER, Almighty and Everlasting God, this unspotted Host, which I, Thine unworthy servant, offer unto Thee, my living and true God, to atone for my countless sins, offenses, and negligences: on behalf of all here present and likewise for all faithful Christians, living and dead, that it may avail both me and them as a means of salvation, unto life everlasting. Amen.

O GOD, ✠ Who in creating man didst exalt his nature very wonderfully and yet more wonderfully didst establish it anew; by the Mystery signified in the mingling of this water and wine, grant us to have part in the Godhead of Him Who hath deigned to become a partaker of our humanity, Jesus Christ, Thy Son, our Lord; Who liveth and reigneth with Thee, in the unity of the Holy Ghost, God. World without end. Amen.

Offerimus tibi, Domine, calicem salutaris, tuam deprecantes clementiam: ut in conspectu divinæ majestatis tuæ, pro nostra et totius mundi salute, cum odore suavitatis ascendat. Amen.

In spiritu humilitatis et in animo contrito suscipiamur a te, Domine: et sic fiat sacrificium nostrum in conspectu tuo hodie, ut placeat tibi, Domine Deus.

Veni, Sanctificator omnipotens æterne Deus: et benedic ✠ hoc sacrificium, tuo sancto nomini præparatum.

Per intercessionem beati Michaelis Archangeli, stantis a dextris altaris incensi, et omnium electorum suorum, incensum istud dignetur Dominus benedicere, ✠ et in odorem suavitatis accipere. Per Christum Dominum nostrum. Amen.

Incensum istud a te benedictum ascendat ad te, Domine: et descendat super nos misericordia tua.

Dirigatur, Domine, oratio mea, sicut incensum, in conspectu tuo: elevatio manuum mearum sacrificium vespertinum.

Pone, Domine, custodiam ori meo, et ostium circumstantiæ labiis meis: ut non declinet cor meum in verba malitiæ, ad excusandas excusationes in peccatis.

Accendat in nobis Dominus ignem sui amoris, et flammam æternæ caritatis. Amen.

WE OFFER UNTO THEE, O Lord, the chalice of salvation, entreating Thy mercy that our offering may ascend with a sweet fragrance in the sight of Thy divine Majesty, for our own salvation, and for that of the whole world. Amen.

HUMBLED IN SPIRIT and contrite of heart, may we find favor with Thee, O Lord: and may our sacrifice be so offered this day in Thy sight as to be pleasing to Thee, O Lord God.

COME THOU, the Sanctifier, Almighty and Everlasting God, and bless ✠ this sacrifice which is prepared for the glory of Thy holy Name.

INCENSING OF THE OFFERINGS AT HIGH MASS

BY THE INTERCESSION of blessed Michael the Archangel, who standeth at the right hand of the Altar of incense, and of all His Elect, may the Lord deign to bless ✠ this incense, and to accept its fragrant sweetness. Through Christ our Lord. Amen.

MAY this incense which Thou hast blessed, O Lord, ascend to Thee, and may Thy mercy descend upon us.

WELCOME as incense-smoke let my prayer rise up before Thee, O Lord. When I lift up my hands, be it as acceptable as the evening sacrifice.

O Lord, set a guard before my mouth, a barrier to fence in my lips. Do not turn my heart toward thoughts of evil, to make excuses for sins.

MAY the Lord enkindle in us the fire of His love and the flame of everlasting charity. Amen.

LAVABO inter innocentes manus meas: et circumdabo altare tuum, Domine. Ut audiam vocem laudis: et enarrem universa mirabilia tua. Domine, dilexi decorem domus tuæ: et locum habitationis gloriæ tuæ. Ne perdas cum impiis, Deus: animam meam, et cum viris sanguinum vitam meam. In quorum manibus iniquitates sunt: dextera eorum repleta est muneribus.

Ego autem in innocentia mea ingressus sum: redime me, et miserere mei. Pes meus stetit in directo: in ecclesiis benedicam te, Domine.

Gloria Patri, et Filio, et Spiritui Sancto. Sicut erat in principio, et nunc, et semper, et in sæcula sæculorum. Amen.

SUSCIPE, SANCTA TRINITAS, hanc oblationem, quam tibi offerimus ob memoriam passionis, resurrectionis, et ascensionis Jesu Christi, Domini nostri: et in honorem beatæ Mariæ semper Virginis, et beati Joannis Baptistæ, et sanctorum Apostolorum Petri et Pauli, et istorum, et omnium Sanctorum: ut illis proficiat ad honorem, nobis autem ad salutem: et illi pro nobis intercedere dignentur in cælis, quorum memoriam agimus in terris. Per eundem Christum Dominum nostrum. Amen.

ORATE, FRATRES: ut meum ac vestrum sacrificium acceptabile fiat apud Deum Patrem omnipotentem.

S. Suscipiat Dominus sacrificium de manibus tuis / ad laudem et gloriam nominis sui, / ad utilitatem quoque nostram, / totiusque Ecclesiæ suae sanctæ.

P. Amen.

Lavabo—Psalm 25:6-12

I WILL WASH MY HANDS among the innocent, and I will encompass Thine Altar, O Lord. That I may hear the voice of praise, and tell of all Thy wondrous works. I have loved, O Lord, the beauty of Thy house, and the place where Thy glory dwelleth. Take not away my soul, O God, with the wicked, nor my life with men of blood. In whose hands are iniquities, their right hand is filled with gifts.

But as for me, I have walked in my innocence; redeem me, and have mercy on me. My foot hath stood in the right way; in the churches I will bless Thee, O Lord.

Glory be to the Father, and to the Son, and to the Holy Ghost. As it was in the beginning, is now, and ever shall be, world without end. Amen.

Prayer to the Most Holy Trinity

RECEIVE, O HOLY TRINITY, this oblation which we make to Thee in memory of the Passion, Resurrection and Ascension of our Lord Jesus Christ; and in honor of Blessed Mary ever Virgin, of blessed John the Baptist, the holy Apostles Peter and Paul, of these and of all the Saints. To them let it bring honor, and to us salvation, and may they whom we are commemorating here on earth deign to plead for us in heaven. Through the same Christ our Lord. Amen.

ORATE FRATRES

PRAY, BRETHREN, that my Sacrifice and yours may be acceptable to God the Father Almighty.

S. May the Lord accept the Sacrifice from thy hands, to the praise and glory of His Name, for our benefit and for that of all His holy Church.

P. Amen.

THE SECRET(S)

Sanctifica, quæsumus, Domine Deus noster, per tui sancti nominis invocationem, hujus oblationis hostiam: et per eam nosmetipsos tibi perfice munus æternum. Per Dominum nostrum Jesum Christum, Filium tuum, qui tecum vivit et regnat, in unitate Spiritus Sancti Deus,

P. Per omnia sæcula sæculorum.
S. Amen.
P. Dominus vobiscum.
S. Et cum spiritu tuo.
P. Sursum corda.
S. Habemus ad Dominum.
P. Gratias agamus Domino Deo nostro.
S. Dignum et justum est.

VERE DIGNUM ET JUSTUM EST, æquum et salutare, nos tibi semper et ubique gratias agere: Domine sancte, Pater omnipotens, æterne Deus: Qui cum unigenito Filio tuo, et Spiritu Sancto, unus es Deus, unus es Dominus: non in unius singularitate personæ, sed in unius Trinitate substantiæ. Quod enim de tua gloria, revelante te, credimus, hoc de Filio tuo, hoc de Spiritu Sancto, sine differentia discretionis sentimus. Ut in confessione veræ sempiternæque Deitatis, et in personis proprietas, et in essentia unitas, et in majestate adoretur æqualitas. Quam laudant Angeli atque Archangeli, Cherubim quoque ac Seraphim: qui non cessant clamare quotidie, una voce dicentes:

SANCTUS, SANCTUS, SANCTUS, Dominus Deus Sabaoth. Pleni sunt cæli et terra gloria tua. Hosanna in excelsis.
✠ Benedictus qui venit in nomine Domini. Hosanna in excelsis.

THE SECRET(S) (Proper)

Sanctify, we beseech Thee, O Lord our God, by the invocation of Thy holy Name, the Sacrifice we offer, and through its means make us ourselves a perfect offering forever. Through our Lord Jesus Christ Thy Son, Who liveth and reigneth with Thee in the unity of the Holy Ghost, God,

P. World without end. **STAND** High Mass

S. Amen.

P. The Lord be with you.

S. And with thy spirit.

P. Lift up your hearts.

S. We have lifted them up to the Lord.

P. Let us give thanks to the Lord our God.

S. It is right and just.

Preface (Of the Most Holy Trinity)

It is truly meet and just, right and profitable for our salvation, that we should at all times and in all places, give thanks unto Thee, O holy Lord, Father Almighty, Everlasting God; Who, together with Thine Only-begotten Son, and the Holy Ghost, art one God, one Lord; not in the oneness of a single Person, but in the Trinity of one substance. For what we believe by Thy revelation of Thy glory, the same do we believe of Thy Son, the same of the Holy Ghost, without difference or inequality. So that in confessing the True and Everlasting Godhead, distinction in Persons, unity in Essence, and equality in Majesty may be adored. Which the Angels and Archangels, the Cherubim also and the Seraphim do praise: who cease not daily to cry out, with one voice saying:

Sanctus

KNEEL

Holy, Holy, Holy, Lord God of Hosts. Heaven and earth are full of Thy Glory. Hosanna in the highest.

✠ Blessed is He Who cometh in the Name of the Lord. Hosanna in the highest.

Canon

TE IGITUR, clementissime Pater, per Jesum Christum Filium tuum, Dominum nostrum, supplices rogamus, ac petimus, uti accepta habeas, et benedicas, hæc ✠ dona, hæc ✠ munera, hæc ✠ sancta sacrificia illibata, in primis, quæ tibi offerimus pro Ecclesia tua sancta catholica: quam pacificare, custodire, adunare, et regere digneris toto orbe terrarum: una cum famulo tuo Papa nostro N. et Antistite nostro N. et omnibus orthodoxis, atque catholicæ et apostolicæ fidei cultoribus.

MEMENTO, DOMINE, famulorum famularumque tuarum N. et N. et omnium circumstantium, quorum tibi fides cognita est, et nota devotio, pro quibus tibi offerimus: vel qui tibi offerunt hoc sacrificium laudis, pro se, suisque omnibus: pro redemptione animarum suarum, pro spe salutis et incolumitatis suæ: tibique reddunt vota sua æterno Deo, vivo et vero.

Canon

Prayers Before Consecration

FOR THE CHURCH

Most merciful Father, we humbly pray and beseech Thee, through Jesus Christ Thy Son, our Lord, to accept and to bless these ✠ gifts, these ✠ presents, these ✠ holy unspotted Sacrifices, which we offer up to Thee, in the first place, for Thy Holy Catholic Church, that it may please Thee to grant her peace, to preserve, unite, and govern her throughout the world; as also for Thy servant N. our Pope, and N. our Bishop, and for all orthodox believers and all who profess the Catholic and Apostolic faith.

FOR THE LIVING

Be mindful, O Lord, of Thy servants and handmaids N. and N. and of all here present, whose faith and devotion are known to Thee, for whom we offer, or who offer up to Thee this Sacrifice of praise for themselves and all those dear to them, for the redemption of their souls and the hope of their safety and salvation: who now pay their vows to Thee, the everlasting, living and true God.

COMMUNICANTES, et memoriam venerantes, in primis gloriosæ semper Virginis Mariæ, Genitricis Dei et Domini nostri Jesu Christi: sed et beati Joseph ejusdem Virginis Sponsi, et beatorum Apostolorum ac Martyrum tuorum, Petri et Pauli, Andreæ, Jacobi, Joannis, Thomæ, Jacobi, Philippi, Bartholomæi, Matthæi, Simonis et Thaddæi: Lini, Cleti, Clementis, Xysti, Cornelii, Cypriani, Laurentii, Chrysogoni, Joannis et Pauli, Cosmæ et Damiani: et omnium Sanctorum tuorum; quorum meritis precibusque concedas, ut in omnibus protectionis tuæ muniamur auxilio. Per eundem Christum Dominum nostrum. Amen.

HANC IGITUR oblationem servitutis nostræ, sed et cunctæ familiæ tuæ, quæsumus, Domine, ut placatus accipias: diesque nostros in tua pace disponas, atque ab æterna damnatione nos eripi, et in electorum tuorum jubeas grege numerari. Per Christum Dominum nostrum. Amen.

QUAM OBLATIONEM TU, Deus, in omnibus, quæsumus, bene✠dictam, adscrip✠tam, ra✠tam, rationabilem, acceptabilemque facere digneris: ut nobis Cor✠pus, et San✠guis fiat dilectissimi Filii tui Domini nostri Jesu Christi.

INVOCATION OF THE SAINTS

In communion with, and honoring the memory in the first place of the glorious ever Virgin Mary Mother of our God and Lord Jesus Christ; also of blessed Joseph, her Spouse; and likewise of Thy blessed Apostles and Martyrs, Peter and Paul, Andrew, James, John, Thomas, James, Philip, Bartholomew, Matthew, Simon and Thaddeus, Linus, Cletus, Clement, Sixtus, Cornelius, Cyprian, Lawrence, Chrysogonus, John and Paul, Cosmas and Damian, and of all Thy Saints. Grant for the sake of their merits and prayers that in all things we may be guarded and helped by Thy protection. Through the same Christ our Lord. Amen.

Prayers at Consecration

OBLATION OF THE VICTIM TO GOD

O Lord, we beseech Thee graciously to accept this oblation of our service and that of Thy whole household. Order our days in Thy peace, and command that we be rescued from eternal damnation and numbered in the flock of Thine elect. Through Christ our Lord. Amen.

Humbly we pray Thee, O God, be pleased to make this same offering wholly blessed, ✠ to consecrate ✠ it and approve ✠ it, making it reasonable and acceptable, so that it may become for us the Body ✠ and Blood ✠ of Thy dearly beloved Son, our Lord Jesus Christ.

The Last Supper Leonardo da Vinci

The Eucharist
Fra Angelico

Qui pridie quam pateretur, accepit panem in sanctas ac venerabiles manus suas, et elevatis oculis in cælum ad te Deum, Patrem suum omnipotentem, tibi gratias agens, bene✠dixit, fregit, deditque discipulis suis, dicens: Accipite, et manducate ex hoc omnes:

HOC EST ENIM CORPUS MEUM.

Simili modo postquam cœnatum est,
accipiens et hunc præclarum Calicem in sanctas ac venerabiles manus suas: item tibi gratias agens, bene✠dixit, deditque discipulis suis, dicens: Accipite, et bibite ex eo omnes:

HIC EST ENIM CALIX SANGUINIS MEI,
NOVI ET ÆTERNI TESTAMENTI:
MYSTERIUM FIDEI:
QUI PRO VOBIS ET PRO MULTIS
EFFUNDETUR IN REMISSIONEM
PECCATORUM.

Hæc quotiescumque feceritis,
in mei memoriam facietis.

Consecration of the Host

Who, the day before He suffered, took bread into His Holy and venerable hands, and having lifted up His eyes to heaven, to Thee, God, His Almighty Father, giving thanks to Thee, blessed it, ✠ broke it, and gave it to His disciples, saying: Take and eat ye all of this:

FOR THIS IS MY BODY.

Consecration of the Wine

In like manner, after He had supped, taking also into His holy and venerable hands this goodly chalice, again giving thanks to Thee, He blessed it, ✠ and gave it to His disciples, saying: Take and drink ye all of this:

FOR THIS IS THE CHALICE OF MY BLOOD,
OF THE NEW AND ETERNAL TESTAMENT:
THE MYSTERY OF FAITH:
WHICH SHALL BE SHED FOR YOU
AND FOR MANY
UNTO THE REMISSION OF SINS.

As often as ye shall do these things,
ye shall do them in remembrance of Me.

UNDE et memores, Domine, nos servi tui, sed et plebs tua sancta, ejusdem Christi Filii tui, Domini nostri, tam beatæ passionis, nec non et ab inferis resurrectionis, sed et in cælos gloriosæ ascensionis: offerimus præclaræ majestati tuæ de tuis donis ac datis, hostiam ✠ puram, hostiam ✠ sanctam, hostiam ✠ immaculatam, Panem ✠ sanctum vitæ æternæ, et Calicem ✠ salutis perpetuæ.

SUPRA quæ propitio ac sereno vultu respicere digneris: et accepta habere, sicuti accepta habere dignatus es munera pueri tui justi Abel, et sacrificium Patriarchæ nostri Abrahæ: et quod tibi obtulit summus sacerdos tuus Melchisedech, sanctum sacrificium, immaculatam hostiam.

SUPPLICES te rogamus, omnipotens Deus: jube hæc perferri per manus sancti Angeli tui in sublime altare tuum, in conspectu divinæ majestatis tuæ: ut quotquot ex hac altaris participatione sacrosanctum Filii tui, Cor✠pus, et San✠guinem sumpserimus, omni benedictione cælesti et gratia repleamur. Per eundem Christum Dominum nostrum. Amen.

MEMENTO etiam, Domine, famulorum famularumque tuarum N. et N. qui nos præcesserunt cum signo fidei, et dormiunt in somno pacis. Ipsis, Domine, et omnibus in Christo quiescentibus, locum refrigerii, lucis et pacis, ut indulgeas, deprecamur. Per eundem Christum Dominum nostrum. Amen.

Prayers After Consecration

TO OFFER THE VICTIM

AND NOW, O Lord, we, Thy servants, and with us all Thy holy people, calling to mind the blessed Passion of this same Christ, Thy Son, our Lord, likewise His Resurrection from the grave, and also His glorious Ascension into heaven, do offer unto Thy most sovereign Majesty out of the gifts Thou hast bestowed upon us, a Victim ✠ which is pure, a Victim ✠ which is holy, a Victim ✠ which is spotless, the holy Bread ✠ of life eternal, and the Chalice ✠ of everlasting Salvation.

TO ASK GOD TO ACCEPT OUR OFFERING

DEIGN to look upon them with a favorable and gracious countenance, and to accept them as Thou didst accept the offerings of Thy just servant Abel, and the sacrifice of our Patriarch Abraham, and that which Thy high priest Melchisedech offered up to Thee, a holy Sacrifice, an immaculate Victim.

FOR BLESSINGS

HUMBLY we beseech Thee, almighty God, to command that these our offerings be carried by the hands of Thy holy Angel to Thine Altar on high, in the sight of Thy divine Majesty, so that those of us who shall receive the most sacred Body ✠ and Blood ✠ of Thy Son by partaking thereof from this Altar may be filled with every grace and heavenly blessing: Through the same Christ our Lord. Amen.

FOR THE DEAD

BE MINDFUL, also, O Lord, of Thy servants and handmaids N. and N. who are gone before us with the sign of faith and who sleep the sleep of peace. To these, O Lord, and to all who rest in Christ, grant, we beseech Thee, a place of refreshment, light and peace. Through the same Christ our Lord. Amen.

NOBIS QUOQUE PECCATORIBUS famulis tuis, de multitudine miserationum tuarum sperantibus, partem aliquam et societatem donare digneris, cum tuis sanctis Apostolis et Martyribus: cum Joanne, Stephano, Matthia, Barnaba, Ignatio, Alexandro, Marcellino, Petro, Felicitate, Perpetua, Agatha, Lucia, Agnete, Cæcilia, Anastasia, et omnibus Sanctis tuis: intra quorum nos consortium, non æstimator meriti, sed veniæ, quæsumus, largitor admitte. Per Christum Dominum nostrum.

PER quem hæc omnia, Domine, semper bona creas, sancti✠ficas, vivi✠ficas, bene✠dicis, et præstas nobis.

PER IP✠SUM, ET CUM IP✠SO, ET IN IP✠SO, est tibi Deo Patri ✠ omnipotenti, in unitate Spiritus ✠Sancti, omnis honor, et gloria.

P. Per omnia sæcula sæculorum.
S. Amen.

Communion

P. Oremus.
Præceptis salutaribus moniti, et divina institutione formati, audemus dicere:

PATER NOSTER, qui es in cælis: Sanctificetur nomen tuum: Adveniat regnum tuum: Fiat voluntas tua, sicut in cælo, et in terra. Panem nostrum quotidianum da nobis hodie: Et dimitte nobis debita nostra, sicut et nos dimittimus debitoribus nostris. Et ne nos inducas in tentationem.
S. Sed libera nos a malo.
P. Amen.

FOR ETERNAL HAPPINESS

To us also Thy sinful servants, who put our trust in the multitude of Thy mercies, vouchsafe to grant some part and fellowship with Thy holy Apostles and Martyrs: with John, Stephen, Matthias, Barnabas, Ignatius, Alexander, Marcellinus, Peter, Felicitas, Perpetua, Agatha, Lucy, Agnes, Cecilia, Anastasia, and all Thy Saints. Into their company we beseech Thee admit us, not considering our merits, but freely pardoning our offenses. Through Christ our Lord.

FINAL DOXOLOGY & MINOR ELEVATION

By whom, O Lord, Thou dost always create, sanctify, ✠ quicken, ✠ bless, ✠ and bestow upon us all these good things.

Through Him, ✠ and with Him, ✠ and in Him, ✠ is unto Thee, God the Father ✠ Almighty, in the unity of the Holy ✠ Ghost, all honor and glory.

P. World without end.
S. Amen.

Communion

STAND
High Mass

PATER NOSTER

P. Let us pray.
Admonished by Thy saving precepts and following Thy divine instruction, we make bold to say:

Our Father, Who art in heaven, hallowed be Thy Name; Thy kingdom come; Thy will be done on earth as it is in heaven. Give us this day our daily bread; and forgive us our trespasses, as we forgive those who trespass against us. And lead us not into temptation.
S. But deliver us from evil.
P. Amen.

Libera nos, quæsumus, Domine, ab omnibus malis, præteritis, præsentibus, et futuris: et intercedente beata et gloriosa semper Virgine Dei Genitrice Maria, cum beatis Apostolis tuis Petro et Paulo, atque Andrea, et omnibus Sanctis,✠ da propitius pacem in diebus nostris: ut ope misericordiæ tuæ adjuti, et a peccato simus semper liberi, et ab omni perturbatione securi.

Per eundem Dominum nostrum Jesum Christum Filium tuum,
Qui tecum vivit et regnat in unitate Spiritus Sancti Deus,

P. Per omnia sæcula sæculorum.
S. Amen.

P. Pax ✠ Domini sit ✠ semper vobis✠cum.
S. Et cum spiritu tuo.

Hæc commixtio, et consecratio Corporis et Sanguinis Domini nostri Jesu Christi, fiat accipientibus nobis in vitam æternam. Amen.

Agnus Dei, qui tollis peccata mundi: miserere nobis.
Agnus Dei, qui tollis peccata mundi: miserere nobis.
Agnus Dei, qui tollis peccata mundi: dona nobis pacem.

Domine Jesu Christe, qui dixisti Apostolis tuis: Pacem relinquo vobis, pacem meam do vobis: ne respicias peccata mea, sed fidem Ecclesiæ tuæ; eamque secundum voluntatem tuam pacificare et coadunare digneris: Qui vivis et regnas Deus per omnia sæcula sæculorum. Amen.

LIBERA NOS

DELIVER US, we beseech Thee, O Lord, from all evils, past, present and to come, and by the intercession of the Blessed and glorious Mary, ever Virgin, Mother of God, together with Thy blessed Apostles Peter and Paul, and Andrew, and all the Saints, ✠ mercifully grant peace in our days, that through the bounteous help of Thy mercy we may be always free from sin, and safe from all disquiet.

BREAKING OF THE HOST

THROUGH the same Jesus Christ, Thy Son our Lord, Who liveth and reigneth with Thee in the unity of the Holy Ghost, God,

P. World without end.
S. Amen.

P. May the peace ✠ of the Lord be ✠ always ✠ with you.
S. And with thy spirit. **KNEEL**

MIXTURE OF THE BODY AND BLOOD

MAY this mingling and hallowing of the Body and Blood of our Lord Jesus Christ be for us who receive it a source of eternal life. Amen.

AGNUS DEI

LAMB OF GOD, Who takest away the sins of the world, have mercy on us.
Lamb of God, Who takest away the sins of the world, have mercy on us.
Lamb of God, Who takest away the sins of the world, grant us peace.

Prayers for Holy Communion

PRAYER FOR PEACE AND FIDELITY

O LORD, Jesus Christ, Who didst say to Thine Apostles: Peace I leave you, My peace I give you: look not upon my sins, but upon the faith of Thy Church; and deign to give her that peace and unity which is agreeable to Thy will: God Who livest and reignest world without end. Amen.

DOMINE Jesu Christe, Fili Dei vivi, qui ex voluntate Patris, cooperante Spiritu Sancto, per mortem tuam mundum vivificasti: libera me per hoc sacrosanctum Corpus et Sanguinem tuum ab omnibus iniquitatibus meis, et universis malis: et fac me tuis semper inhærere mandatis, et a te numquam separari permittas: Qui cum eodem Deo Patre, et Spiritu Sancto vivis et regnas Deus in sæcula sæculorum. Amen.

PERCEPTIO Corporis tui, Domine Jesu Christe, quod ego indignus sumere præsumo, non mihi proveniat in judicium et condemnationem: sed pro tua pietate prosit mihi ad tutamentum mentis et corporis, et ad medelam percipiendam: Qui vivis et regnas cum Deo Patre in unitate Spiritus Sancti Deus, per omnia sæcula sæculorum. Amen.

PANEM cælestem accipiam, et nomen Domini invocabo.

DOMINE, non sum dignus, ut intres sub tectum meum: sed tantum dic verbo, et sanabitur anima mea. (Said three times)

CORPUS Domini nostri Jesu Christi custodiat animam meam in vitam æternam. Amen.

QUID retribuam Domino pro omnibus quæ retribuit mihi? Calicem salutaris accipiam, et nomen Domini invocabo. Laudans invocabo Dominum, et ab inimicis meis salvus ero.

SANGUIS Domini nostri Jesu Christi custodiat animam meam in vitam æternam. Amen.

PRAYER FOR HOLINESS

O Lord Jesus Christ, Son of the living God, Who, by the will of the Father and the cooperation of the Holy Ghost, hast by Thy death given life to the world: deliver me by this, Thy most sacred Body and Blood, from all my iniquities and from every evil; make me cling always to Thy commandments, and permit me never to be separated from Thee. Who with the same God, the Father and the Holy Ghost, livest and reignest God, world without end. Amen.

PRAYER FOR GRACE

Let not the partaking of Thy Body, O Lord Jesus Christ, which I, though unworthy, presume to receive, turn to my judgment and condemnation; but through Thy mercy may it be unto me a safeguard and a healing remedy both of soul and body. Who livest and reignest with God the Father, in the unity of the Holy Ghost, God, world without end. Amen.

COMMUNION OF THE PRIEST

I will take the Bread of Heaven, and will call upon the name of the Lord.

Lord, I am not worthy that Thou shouldst enter under my roof; but only say the word, and my soul shall be healed. (Said three times)

May the Body of our Lord Jesus Christ preserve my soul unto life everlasting. Amen.

What return shall I make to the Lord for all the things that He hath given unto me? I will take the chalice of salvation, and call upon the Name of the Lord. I will call upon the Lord and give praise: and I shall be saved from mine enemies.

May the Blood of our Lord Jesus Christ preserve my soul unto life everlasting. Amen.

Confiteor (see page 8)

Misereatur vestri omnipotens Deus, et dimissis peccatis vestris, perducat vos ad vitam æternam. S. Amen.

Indulgentiam, ✠ absolutionem et remissionem peccatorum vestrorum tribuat vobis omnipotens, et misericors Dominus.
S. Amen.

Ecce Agnus Dei, ecce qui tollit peccata mundi.

Domine, non sum dignus, ut intres sub tectum meum: sed tantum dic verbo, et sanabitur anima mea. (said three times)

Corpus Domini nostri Jesu Christi custodiat animam tuam in vitam æternam. Amen.

Quod ore sumpsimus, Domine, pura mente capiamus: et de munere temporali fiat nobis remedium sempiternum.

Corpus tuum, Domine, quod sumpsi, et Sanguis, quem potavi, adhæreat visceribus meis: et præsta; ut in me non remaneat scelerum macula, quem pura et sancta refecerunt sacramenta: Qui vivis et regnas in sæcula sæculorum. Amen.

May Almighty God have mercy on you, forgive you your sins, and bring you to life everlasting.
S. Amen.

May the Almighty and Merciful Lord grant you pardon, ✠ absolution, and remission of your sins.
S. Amen.

BEHOLD the Lamb of God, behold Him Who taketh away the sins of the world.

LORD, I am not worthy that Thou shouldst enter under my roof; but only say the word, and my soul shall be healed. (said three times)

MAY the Body of our Lord Jesus Christ preserve your soul unto life everlasting. Amen.

Prayers after Communion

ABLUTIONS

GRANT, O Lord, that what we have taken with our mouth, we may receive with a pure mind; and that from a temporal gift it may become for us an everlasting remedy.

MAY THY BODY, O Lord, which I have received and Thy Blood which I have drunk, cleave to my inmost parts, and grant that no stain of sin remain in me; whom these pure and holy Sacraments have refreshed. Who livest and reignest world without end. Amen.

COMMUNION VERSE

Benedicimus Deum cæli, et coram omnibus viventibus confitebimur ei: quia fecit nobiscum misericordiam suam.

P. Dominus vobiscum.
S. Et cum spiritu tuo.
P. Oremus.

POSTCOMMUNION(S)

Proficiat nobis ad salutem corporis et animæ, Domine Deus noster, hujus sacramenti susceptio: et sempiternæ sanctæ Trinitatis, ejusdemque individuæ unitatis confessio. Per Dominum nostrum Jesum Christum, Filium tuum, qui tecum vivit et regnat, in unitate Spiritus Sancti, Deus, per omnia sæcula sæculorum.
S. Amen.

P. Dominus vobiscum.
S. Et cum spiritu tuo.

P. Ite, Missa est.
S. Deo gratias.

P. Benedicamus Domino.
S. Deo gratias.

P. Requiescant in pace.
S. Amen.

PLACEAT TIBI, sancta Trinitas, obsequium servitutis meæ: et præsta; ut sacrificium, quod oculis tuæ majestatis indignus obtuli, tibi sit acceptabile, mihique, et omnibus, pro quibus illud obtuli, sit, te miserante, propitiabile. Per Christum Dominum nostrum. Amen.

BENEDICAT VOS OMNIPOTENS DEUS, Pater,
et Filius, ✠ et Spiritus Sanctus.
S. Amen.

THE COMMUNION VERSE (Proper)

We bless the God of Heaven, and before all the living we will praise Him; because He hath shown His mercy to us.

P. The Lord be with you.
S. And with thy spirit.
P. Let us pray.

STAND
High Mass

THE POSTCOMMUNION(S) (Proper)

May the reception of this Sacrament, O Lord our God, and the confession of the holy and eternal Trinity and of its undivided Unity, profit us to the salvation of body and soul. Through our Lord Jesus Christ Thy Son, Who liveth and reigneth with Thee in the unity of the Holy Ghost, God, for ever and ever.
S. Amen.

P. The Lord be with you.
S. And with thy spirit.

THE DISMISSAL

P. Go, the Mass is ended.
S. Thanks be to God.
or:
P. Let us bless the Lord.
S. Thanks be to God.
or:
P. May they rest in peace.
S. Amen.

THE LAST BLESSING

KNEEL

MAY THE TRIBUTE of my homage be pleasing to Thee, O most holy Trinity. Grant that the Sacrifice which I, unworthy as I am, have offered in the presence of Thy Majesty, may be acceptable to Thee. Through Thy mercy may it bring forgiveness to me and to all for whom I have offered it. Through Christ our Lord. Amen.

MAY ALMIGHTY GOD BLESS YOU: the Father,
the Son, ✠ and the Holy Ghost.
S. Amen.

P. Dominus vobiscum.
S. Et cum spiritu tuo.
P. ✠ Initium sancti Evangelii secundum Joannem.
S. Gloria tibi, Domine.

In principio erat Verbum, et Verbum erat apud Deum, et Deus erat Verbum. Hoc erat in principio apud Deum. Omnia per ipsum facta sunt: et sine ipso factum est nihil, quod factum est: in ipso vita erat, et vita erat lux hominum: et lux in tenebris lucet, et tenebræ eam non comprehenderunt.

Fuit homo missus a Deo, cui nomen erat Joannes. Hic venit in testimonium, ut testimonium perhiberet de lumine, ut omnes crederent per illum. Non erat ille lux, sed ut testimonium perhiberet de lumine.

Erat lux vera, quae illuminat omnem hominem venientem in hunc mundum. In mundo erat, et mundus per ipsum factus est, et mundus eum non cognovit. In propria venit, et sui eum non receperunt. Quotquot autem receperunt eum, dedit eis potestatem filios Dei fieri, his, qui credunt in nomine ejus: qui non ex sanguinibus, neque ex voluntate carnis, neque ex voluntate viri, sed ex Deo nati sunt.

ET VERBUM CARO FACTUM EST,
et habitavit in nobis: et vidimus gloriam ejus, gloriam quasi Unigeniti a Patre, plenum gratiæ et veritatis.

S. Deo gratias.

LAST GOSPEL **STAND**

P. The Lord be with you.
S. And with thy spirit.
P. ✠ The beginning of the holy Gospel according to Saint John.
S. Glory be to Thee, O Lord.

In the beginning was the Word, and the Word was with God, and the Word was God. The same was in the beginning with God. All things were made by Him, and without Him was made nothing that was made. In Him was life, and the life was the Light of men: and the Light shineth in darkness, and the darkness did not comprehend it.

There was a man sent from God, whose name was John. This man came for a witness, to bear witness of the Light, that all men through Him might believe. He was not the Light, but was to bear witness of the Light.

That was the true Light, which enlighteneth every man that cometh into this world. He was in the world, and the world was made by Him, and the world knew Him not. He came unto His own, and His own received Him not. But as many as received Him, to them He gave power to become the sons of God; to them that believe in His name: who are born, not of blood, nor of the will of the flesh, nor of the will of man, but of God.

AND THE WORD WAS MADE FLESH, **GENUFLECT**
and dwelt among us, and we saw His glory, the glory as of the Only-begotten of the Father, full of grace and truth.

S. Thanks be to God.

PRAYERS AFTER LOW MASS

KNEEL

Priest: HAIL MARY, full of grace, the Lord is with thee; blessed art thou among women, and blessed is the Fruit of thy womb, Jesus.

All: Holy Mary, Mother of God, pray for us sinners, now and at the hour of our death. Amen.

HAIL, HOLY QUEEN, Mother of Mercy, our life, our sweetness, and our hope. To thee do we cry, poor banished children of Eve. To thee do we send up our sighs, mourning and weeping in this vale of tears. Turn then, most gracious Advocate, thine eyes of mercy toward us. And after this our exile, show unto us the blessed Fruit of thy womb, Jesus. O clement, O loving, O sweet Virgin Mary.

P. Pray for us, O holy Mother of God.
All. That we may be made worthy of the promises of Christ.

P. Let us pray.

O GOD, our refuge and our strength, look down with favor upon Thy people who cry to Thee; and by the intercession of the glorious and Immaculate Virgin Mary, Mother of God, of St. Joseph her Spouse, of Thy blessed Apostles Peter and Paul, and of all the Saints, mercifully and graciously hear the prayers which we pour forth for the conversion of sinners, and for the liberty and exaltation of our holy Mother the Church. Through the same Christ our Lord.

All. Amen.

SAINT MICHAEL, the Archangel, defend us in battle; be our protection against the wickedness and snares of the devil. May God rebuke him, we humbly pray: and do thou, O Prince of the heavenly host, by the power of God, thrust down to hell Satan and all the evil spirits who roam through the world seeking the ruin of souls. Amen.

P. Most Sacred Heart of Jesus,
All. Have mercy on us.

Trinity
Masaccio

The Pentecost
Titian

Nuptial Mass

1962 Typical Edition

Betrothal of the Virgin
Raphael

The Marriage Service

P. N. wilt thou take N. here present, for thy lawful wife, according to the rite of our holy Mother the Church?
R. I will.

P. N. wilt thou take N. here present, for thy lawful husband, according to the rite of our holy Mother the Church?
B. I will.

I, N., take thee, N., for my lawful wife, to have and to hold, from this day forward, for better, for worse, for richer, for poorer, in sickness and in health, until death do us part.

I, N. take thee, N. for my lawful husband, to have and to hold, from this day forward, for better, for worse, for richer, for poorer, in sickness and in health, until death do us part.

I join you together in Holy Matrimony, in the name of the Father, ✠ and of the Son, and of the Holy Ghost. Amen.

P. Adjutorium nostrum in nomine Domini.
R. Qui fecit cælum et terram.
P. Domine, exaudi orationem meam.
R. Et clamor meus ad te veniat.
P. Dominus vobiscum.
R. Et cum spiritu tuo.
P. Oremus.
Benedic, ✠ Domine, annulum hunc, quem nos tuo nomine benedicimus, ✠ ut quæ eum gestaverit, fidelitatem integram suo sponso tenens, in pace et voluntate tua permaneat atque in mutua caritate semper vivat. Per Christum Dominum nostrum. Amen.

In nomine Patris, et Filii, et Spiritus Sancti. Amen.

P. Confirma hoc, Deus, quod operatus es in nobis.
R. A templo sancto tuo, quod est in Jerusalem.
P. Kyrie eleison. Christe eleison. Kyrie eleison.
P. Pater noster (silently).
P. Et ne nos inducas in tentationem. (audibly)
R. Sed libera nos a malo.
P. Salvos fac servos tuos.
R. Deus meus, sperantes in te.
P. Mitte eis, Domine, auxilium de sancto.
R. Et de Sion tuere eos.
P. Esto eis, Domine, turris fortitudinis.
R. A facie inimici.
P. Domine, exaudi orationem meam.
R. Et clamor meus ad te veniat.
P. Dominus vobisum.
R. Et cum spiritu tuo.
P. Oremus.
Respice, quæsumus, Domine, super hos famulos tuos et institutis tuis, quibus propagationem humani generis ordinasti, benignus assiste, ut qui te auctore junguntur, te auxiliante serventur. Per Christum Dominum nostrum. Amen.

P. Our help is in the name of the Lord.
R. Who hath made heaven and earth.
P. O Lord, hear my prayer.
R. And let my cry come unto Thee.
P. The Lord be with you.
R. And with thy spirit.
P. Let us pray.
Bless ✠ O Lord, this ring, which we bless ✠ in Thy name, that she who shall wear it keeping true faith unto her spouse, may abide in Thy peace and in obedience to Thy will and ever live in mutual love. Through Christ our Lord. Amen.

With this ring I thee wed and I plight unto thee my troth.

In the name of the Father, ✠ and of the Son, and of the Holy Ghost. Amen.
P. Confirm, O God, that which Thou hast wrought in us.
R. From Thy holy temple, which is in Jerusalem.
P. Lord, have mercy. Christ, have mercy. Lord, have mercy.
P. Our Father, etc. (silently)
P. And lead us not into temptation. (audibly)
R. But deliver us from evil.
P. Save Thy servants.
R. Who hope in Thee, O my God.
P. Send them help, O Lord, from Thy holy place.
R. And defend them out of Sion.
P. Be unto them, Lord, a tower of strength.
R. From the face of the enemy.
P. O Lord, hear my prayer.
R. And let my cry come unto Thee.
P. The Lord be with you.
R. And with thy spirit.
P. Let us pray.
Look down with favor, O Lord, we beseech Thee, upon these Thy servants, and graciously protect this Thine ordinance, whereby Thou hast provided for the propagation of mankind; that they who are joined together by Thine authority may be preserved by Thy help; through Christ our Lord. Amen.

ORDO MISSÆ
MASS OF THE CATECHUMENS

In nomine Patris, ✠ et Filii, et Spiritus Sancti. Amen.
P. Introibo ad altare Dei.
S. Ad Deum qui lætificat juventutem meam.

Judica Me—Psalm 42

Judica me, Deus, et discerne causam meam de gente non sancta: ab homine iniquo, et doloso erue me.

S. Quia tu es, Deus, fortitudo mea: / quare me repulisti, / et quare tristis incedo, / dum affligit me inimicus?

P. Emitte lucem tuam, et veritatem tuam: ipsa me deduxerunt, et adduxerunt in montem sanctum tuum, et in tabernacula tua.

S. Et introibo ad altare Dei: / ad Deum qui lætificat juventutem meam.

P. Confitebor tibi in cithara, Deus, Deus meus: quare tristis es, anima mea, et quare conturbas me?

S. Spera in Deo, / quoniam adhuc confitebor illi: salutare vultus mei, / et Deus meus.

P. Gloria Patri, et Filio, et Spiritui Sancto.

S. Sicut erat in principio et nunc, et semper, / et in sæcula sæculorum. Amen.

THE ORDINARY OF THE MASS

MASS OF THE CATECHUMENS

KNEEL

IN THE NAME OF THE FATHER, ✠ and of the Son,
and of the Holy Ghost. Amen.
Priest: I will go in unto the Altar of God.
Server: To God, Who giveth joy to my youth.

Psalm 42—Judica Me

JUDGE ME, O God, and distinguish my cause from the nation that is not holy: deliver me from the unjust and deceitful man.

S. For Thou, O God, art my strength: why hast Thou cast me off? and why do I go sorrowful whilst the enemy afflicteth me?

P. Send forth Thy light and Thy truth: they have led me and brought me unto Thy holy hill, and into Thy tabernacles.

S. And I will go in unto the Altar of God: unto God, Who giveth joy to my youth.

P. I will praise Thee upon the harp, O God, my God: why art thou sad, O my soul? and why dost thou disquiet me?

S. Hope thou in God, for I will yet praise Him: Who is the salvation of my countenance, and my God.

P. Glory be to the Father, and to the Son, and to the Holy Ghost.

S. As it was in the beginning, is now, and ever shall be, world without end. Amen.

P. Introibo ad altare Dei.
S. Ad Deum qui lætificat juventutem meam.
P. Adjutorium nostrum ✠ in nomine Domini.
S. Qui fecit cælum et terram.
P. Confiteor Deo omnipotenti, etc. (as below)
S. Misereatur tui omnipotens Deus, / et dimissis peccatis tuis, / perducat te ad vitam æternam.
P. Amen.

CONFITEOR DEO OMNIPOTENTI, / beatæ Mariæ semper Virgini, / beato Michaeli Archangelo, / beato Joanni Baptistæ, / sanctis Apostolis Petro et Paulo, / omnibus Sanctis, et tibi, Pater: / quia peccavi nimis cogitatione, verbo et opere: / mea culpa, mea culpa, mea maxima culpa. / Ideo precor beatam Mariam semper Virginem, / beatum Michaelem Archangelum, / beatum Joannem Baptistam, / sanctos Apostolos Petrum et Paulum, / omnes Sanctos, et te, Pater, / orare pro me ad Dominum Deum nostrum.

P. Misereatur vestri omnipotens Deus, et dimissis peccatis vestris, perducat vos ad vitam æternam.
S. Amen.
P. Indulgentiam, ✠ absolutionem, et remissionem peccatorum nostrorum tribuat nobis omnipotens et misericors Dominus.
S. Amen.

P. Deus, tu conversus vivificabis nos.
S. Et plebs tua lætabitur in te.
P. Ostende nobis, Domine, misericordiam tuam.
S. Et salutare tuum da nobis.
P. Domine, exaudi orationem meam.
S. Et clamor meus ad te veniat.
P. Dominus vobiscum.
S. Et cum spiritu tuo.

P. I will go in unto the Altar of God.
S. Unto God, Who giveth joy to my youth.
P. Our help ✠ is in the Name of the Lord.
S. Who hath made heaven and earth.
P. I confess to Almighty God, etc. (as below)
S. May Almighty God have mercy upon you, forgive you your sins, and bring you to life everlasting.
P. Amen.

I CONFESS TO ALMIGHTY GOD, to blessed Mary ever Virgin, to blessed Michael the Archangel, to blessed John the Baptist, to the holy Apostles Peter and Paul, to all the Saints, and to you, Father, that I have sinned exceedingly, in thought, word and deed: through my fault, through my fault, through my most grievous fault. Therefore I beseech blessed Mary ever Virgin, blessed Michael the Archangel, blessed John the Baptist, the holy Apostles Peter and Paul, all the Saints, and you, Father, to pray to the Lord our God for me.

P. May Almighty God have mercy upon you,
forgive you your sins, and bring you to life everlasting.
S. Amen.
P. May the Almighty and merciful God grant
us pardon, ✠ absolution, and remission of
our sins.
S. Amen.

P. Thou wilt turn, O God, and bring us to life.
S. And Thy people shall rejoice in Thee.
P. Show us, O Lord, Thy mercy.
S. And grant us Thy salvation.
P. O Lord, hear my prayer.
S. And let my cry come unto Thee.
P. The Lord be with you.
S. And with thy spirit.

P. Oremus.

AUFER a nobis, quæsumus, Domine, iniquitates nostras: ut ad Sancta sanctorum puris mereamur mentibus introire. Per Christum Dominum nostrum. Amen.

ORAMUS TE, Domine, per merita Sanctorum tuorum, quorum reliquiæ hic sunt, et omnium Sanctorum: ut indulgere digneris omnia peccata mea. Amen.

THE INTROIT Tobias 7:15, 8:19

Deus, Israel, conjungat vos: et ipse sit vobiscum qui misertus est duobus unicis: et nunc, Domine, fac eos plenius benedicere te. Beati omnes qui timent Dominum: qui ambulant in viis ejus.

Gloria Patri, et Filio, et Spiritui Sancto. Sicut erat in principio, et nunc, et semper: et in sæcula sæculorum. Amen.

Deus, Israel, conjungat vos: et ipse sit vobiscum qui misertus est duobus unicis: et nunc, Domine, fac eos plenius benedicere te.

P. KYRIE, eleison.
S. Kyrie, eleison.
P. Kyrie, eleison.
S. Christe, eleison.
P. Christe, eleison.
S. Christe, eleison.
P. Kyrie, eleison.
S. Kyrie, eleison.
P. Kyrie, eleison.

P. Let us pray.

The Priest Ascends the Altar

TAKE AWAY from us our iniquities, we entreat Thee, O Lord, that with pure minds we may worthily enter into the Holy of Holies. Through Christ our Lord. Amen.

WE BESEECH THEE, O Lord, by the merits of Thy Saints, whose relics are here, and of all the Saints, that Thou wilt deign to pardon me all my sins. Amen.

THE INTROIT (Proper)

May the God of Israel join you together: and may He be with you, who was merciful to two only children: and now, O Lord, make them bless Thee more fully. Blessed are all they that fear the Lord, that walk in His ways.

Glory be to the Father, and to the Son, and to the Holy Ghost. As it was in the beginning, is now, and ever shall be, world without end. Amen.

May the God of Israel join you together: and may He be with you, who was merciful to two only children: and now, O Lord, make them bless Thee more fully.

Kyrie Eleison

P. LORD, have mercy on us.
S. Lord, have mercy on us.
P. Lord, have mercy on us.
S. Christ, have mercy on us.
P. Christ, have mercy on us.
S. Christ, have mercy on us.
P. Lord, have mercy on us.
S. Lord, have mercy on us.
P. Lord, have mercy on us.

Gloria in excelsis Deo, / et in terra pax hominibus / bonæ voluntatis. / Laudamus te. / Benedicimus te. / Adoramus te. / Glorificamus te. / Gratias agimus tibi / propter magnam gloriam tuam. / Domine Deus, / Rex cælestis, / Deus Pater omnipotens. /Domine Fili unigenite, / Jesu Christe. / Domine Deus, / Agnus Dei, / Filius Patris. / Qui tollis peccata mundi, / miserere nobis. / Qui tollis peccata mundi, / suscipe deprecationem nostram. / Qui sedes ad dexteram Patris, / miserere nobis. / Quoniam tu solus Sanctus. / Tu solus Dominus. / Tu solus Altissimus, Jesu Christe. / Cum Sancto Spiritu, ✠ / in gloria Dei Patris. / Amen.

P. Dominus vobiscum.
S. Et cum spiritu tuo.
P. Oremus.

THE COLLECT

Exaudi nos, omnipotens et misericors Deus: ut, quod nostro ministratur officio, tua benedictione potius impleatur. Per Dominum nostrum Jesum Christum, Filium tuum, qui tecum vivit et regnat, in unitate Spiritus Sancti, Deus, per omnia sæcula sæculorum. S. Amen.

THE EPISTLE

Ephesians 5:22-33

Fratres: Mulieres viris suis subditæ sint, sicut Domino: quoniam vir caput est mulieris: sicut Christus caput est Ecclesiæ: Ipse, salvator corporis ejus: Sed sicut Ecclesia subjecta est Christo, ita et mulieres viris suis in omnibus. Viri, diligite uxores vestras, sicut et Christus dilexit Ecclesiam, et seipsum tradidit pro ea, ut illam sanctificaret, mundans lavacro aquæ in verbo vitæ, ut

STAND
High Mass

Gloria in Excelsis

Glory be to God on high. And on earth peace to men of good will. We praise Thee. We bless Thee. We adore Thee. We glorify Thee. We give Thee thanks for Thy great glory. Lord God, heavenly King, God the Father Almighty. Lord Jesus Christ, Only-begotten Son, Lord God, Lamb of God, Son of the Father. Thou Who takest away the sins of the world, have mercy on us. Thou Who takest away the sins of the world, receive our prayer. Thou Who sittest at the right hand of the Father, have mercy on us. For Thou alone art holy. Thou alone art the Lord. Thou alone, O Jesus Christ, art most high. With the Holy Ghost, ✠ in the glory of God the Father. Amen.

P. The Lord be with you.
S. And with thy spirit.
P. Let us pray.

THE COLLECT (Proper)

Graciously hear us, almighty and merciful God, that what is done by our ministry may be abundantly fulfilled by Thy blessing. Through our Lord Jesus Christ Thy Son, Who liveth and reigneth with Thee in the unity of the Holy Ghost, God, for ever and ever.
S. Amen.

SIT
High Mass

THE EPISTLE (Proper)

Brethren: Let women be subject to their husbands as to the Lord; for the husband is the head of the wife, as Christ is the head of the Church. He is the saviour of His body. Therefore, as the Church is subject to Christ, so also let the wives be to their husbands in all things. Husbands, love your wives, as Christ also loved the Church, and delivered Himself up for it: that He might sanctify it, cleansing it by the

exhiberet ipse sibi gloriosam Ecclesiam, non habentem maculam, aut rugam, aut aliquid hujusmodi, sed ut sit sancta et immaculata. Ita et viri debent diligere uxores suas, ut corpora sua. Qui suam uxorem diligit, seipsum diligit. Nemo enim umquam carnem suam odio habuit: sed nutrit, et fovet eam, sicut et Christus Ecclesiam: quia membra sumus corporis ejus, de carne ejus, et de ossibus ejus. Propter hoc relinquet homo patrem et matrem suam, et adhærebit uxori suæ: et erunt duo in carne una. Sacramentum hoc magnum est, ego autem dico in Christo, et in Ecclesia. Verumtamen et vos singuli, unusquisque uxorem suam, sicut seipsum diligat: uxor autem timeat virum suum.
S. Deo gratias.

THE GRADUAL

Uxor tua sicut vitis abundans in lateribus domus tuæ. Filii tui sicut novellæ olivarum in circuitu mensæ tuæ.

Alleluia, alleluia. Mittat vobis Dominus auxilium de sancto: et de Sion tueatur vos. Alleluia.

TRACT

Ecce sic benedicetur omnis homo, qui timet Dominum. Benedicat tibi Dominus ex Sion: et videas bona Jerusalem omnibus diebus vitæ tuæ. Et videas filios filiorum tuorum: pax super Israel.

EASTERTIME ALLELUIA

Alleluia, alleluia. Mittat vobis Dominus auxilium de sancto : et de Sion tueatur vos.

Alleluia. Benedicat vobis Dominus ex Sion: qui fecit cælum et terram. Alleluia.

laver of water in the word of life; that He might present it to Himself a glorious Church, not having spot or wrinkle, or any such thing, but that it should be holy and without blemish. So also ought men to love their wives as their own bodies. He that loveth his wife loveth himself: for no man ever hated his own flesh, but nourisheth and cherisheth it; as also Christ doth the Church: for we are members of His body, of His flesh, and of His bones. For this cause shall a man leave his father and mother, and shall cleave to his wife; and they shall be two in one flesh. This is a great sacrament, but I speak in Christ and in the Church. Nevertheless, let every one of you in particular love his wife as himself, and let the wife fear her husband.

S. Thanks be to God.

THE GRADUAL (Proper)

Thy wife shall be as a fruitful vine on the sides of thy house. Thy children as olive plants round about thy table.

Alleluia, alleluia. May the Lord send you help from the sanctuary, and defend you out of Sion. Alleluia.

TRACT

Behold, thus shall the man be blessed that feareth the Lord. May the Lord bless thee out of Sion; and mayest thou see the good things of Jerusalem all the days of thy life. And mayest thou see thy children's children: peace upon Israel.

EASTERTIME ALLELUIA

Alleluia, alleluia. May the Lord send you help from the sanctuary, and defend you out of Sion.

Alleluia. May the Lord out of Sion bless you, who hath made heaven and earth. Alleluia.

MUNDA COR MEUM ac labia mea, omnipotens Deus, qui labia Isaiæ Prophetæ calculo mundasti ignito: ita me tua grata miseratione dignare mundare, ut sanctum Evangelium tuum digne valeam nuntiare. Per Christum Dominum nostrum. Amen.

Jube, Domine, benedicere.

Dominus sit in corde meo, et in labiis meis: ut digne et competenter annuntiem Evangelium suum. Amen.

THE GOSPEL Matthew 19:3-6

P. Dominus vobiscum.
S. Et cum spiritu tuo.
P. ✠ Sequentia sancti Evangelii secundum Matthæum.
S. Gloria tibi, Domine.

In illo tempore: Accesserunt ad Jesum pharisæi tentantes eum, et dicentes: Si licet homini dimittere uxorem suam quacumque ex causa? Qui respondens, ait eis: Non legistis, quia qui fecit hominem ab initio, masculum et feminam fecit eos? et dixit: Propter hoc dimittet homo patrem, et matrem, et adhærebit uxori suæ, et erunt duo in carne una. Itaque jam non sunt duo, sed una caro. Quod ergo Deus conjunxit, homo non separet.

S. Laus tibi, Christe.

P. Per evangelica dicta, deleantur nostra delicta.

Munda Cor Meum

Cleanse my heart and my lips, O Almighty God, Who didst cleanse the lips of the prophet Isaias with a burning coal; through Thy gracious mercy so purify me that I may worthily proclaim Thy holy Gospel. Through Christ our Lord. Amen.

Grant, O Lord, Thy blessing.

May the Lord be in my heart and on my lips that I may worthily and fittingly proclaim His Gospel. Amen.

THE GOSPEL

STAND

P. The Lord be with you.
S. And with thy spirit.
P. ✠ The continuation of the holy Gospel according to St. Matthew.
S. Glory be to Thee, O Lord.

At that time: the pharisees came to Jesus, tempting Him and saying: Is it lawful for a man to put away his wife for every cause? Who, answering, said to them: Have ye not read that He Who made man from the beginning, made them male and female? And He said: "For this cause shall a man leave father and mother, and shall cleave to his wife, and they two shall be in one flesh. Therefore now they are not two but one flesh. What therefore God hath joined together, let no man put asunder."
S. Praise be to Thee, O Christ.

P. By the words of the Gospel may our sins be blotted out.

Sermon

SIT

CREDO IN UNUM DEUM, / Patrem omnipotentem, / factorem cæli et terræ, / visibilium omnium et invisibilium. / Et in unum Dominum Jesum Christum, / Filium Dei unigenitum. / Et ex Patre natum / ante omnia sæcula. / Deum de Deo, / lumen de lumine, / Deum verum de Deo vero. / Genitum, non factum, / consubstantialem Patri: / per quem omnia facta sunt. / Qui propter nos homines / et propter nostram salutem / descendit de cælis. / (here all kneel)

ET INCARNATUS EST DE SPIRITU SANCTO / EX MARIA VIRGINE: / ET HOMO FACTUS EST. (rise)

Crucifixus etiam pro nobis: / sub Pontio Pilato / passus, et sepultus est. / Et resurrexit tertia die, / secundum Scripturas. / Et ascendit in cælum: / sedet ad dexteram Patris. / Et iterum venturus est cum gloria / judicare vivos et mortuos: / cujus regni non erit finis. /

Et in Spiritum Sanctum, / Dominum et vivificantem: / qui ex Patre, Filioque procedit. / Qui cum Patre, et Filio / simul adoratur, / et conglorificatur: / qui locutus est per Prophetas./ Et unam, sanctam, catholicam / et apostolicam Ecclesiam. / Confiteor unum baptisma / in remissionem peccatorum. / Et expecto resurrectionem mortuorum. / Et vitam ✠ venturi sæculi. /Amen.

P. Dominus vobiscum.
S. Et cum spiritu tuo.
P. Oremus.

Nicene Creed

STAND

I BELIEVE IN ONE GOD, the Father Almighty, Maker of heaven and earth, and of all things visible and invisible. And in one Lord Jesus Christ, the Only-begotten Son of God. Born of the Father before all ages. God of God, Light of Light, true God of true God. Begotten, not made: consubstantial with the Father; by Whom all things were made. Who for us men, and for our salvation, came down from heaven. (here all kneel)

GENUFLECT

AND WAS INCARNATE BY THE HOLY GHOST OF THE VIRGIN MARY: AND WAS MADE MAN. (rise)

He was crucified also for us, suffered under Pontius Pilate, and was buried. And on the third day He rose again according to the Scriptures. And He ascended into heaven, and sitteth at the right hand of the Father. And He shall come again with glory to judge the living and the dead: of Whose kingdom there shall be no end.

And in the Holy Ghost, the Lord and Giver of Life: Who proceedeth from the Father and the Son. Who together with the Father and the Son is adored and glorified: Who spoke through the Prophets. And in One, Holy, Catholic and Apostolic Church. I confess one Baptism for the remission of sins. And I look for the resurrection of the dead, and the life ✠ of the world to come. Amen.

STAND

P. The Lord be with you.
S. And with thy spirit.
P. Let us pray.

MASS OF THE FAITHFUL

Offertory

THE OFFERTORY

In te speravi, Domine: dixi: Tu es Deus meus: in manibus tuis tempora mea. (T.P. Alleluia.)

Suscipe, sancte Pater, omnipotens æterne Deus, hanc immaculatam hostiam, quam ego indignus famulus tuus offero tibi Deo meo vivo et vero, pro innumerabilibus peccatis, et offensionibus, et negligentiis meis, et pro omnibus circumstantibus, sed et pro omnibus fidelibus christianis vivis atque defunctis: ut mihi et illis proficiat ad salutem in vitam aeternam. Amen.

Deus, ✠ qui humanæ substantiæ dignitatem mirabiliter condidisti et mirabilius reformasti: da nobis, per hujus aquæ et vini mysterium, ejus divinitatis esse consortes, qui humanitatis nostræ fieri dignatus est particeps, Jesus Christus, Filius tuus, Dominus noster: Qui tecum vivit et regnat in unitate Spiritus Sancti Deus: per omnia sæcula sæculorum. Amen.

MASS OF THE FAITHFUL
Offertory

THE OFFERTORY (Proper)

SIT

In Thee, O Lord, have I hoped; I said, Thou art my God; my times are in Thy hands. (P.T. Alleluia.)

Offering of the Bread and Wine

ACCEPT, O HOLY FATHER, Almighty and Everlasting God, this unspotted Host, which I, Thine unworthy servant, offer unto Thee, my living and true God, to atone for my countless sins, offenses, and negligences: on behalf of all here present and likewise for all faithful Christians, living and dead, that it may avail both me and them as a means of salvation, unto life everlasting. Amen.

O GOD, ✠ Who in creating man didst exalt his nature very wonderfully and yet more wonderfully didst establish it anew; by the Mystery signified in the mingling of this water and wine, grant us to have part in the Godhead of Him Who hath deigned to become a partaker of our humanity, Jesus Christ, Thy Son, our Lord; Who liveth and reigneth with Thee, in the unity of the Holy Ghost, God. World without end. Amen.

OFFERIMUS TIBI, Domine, calicem salutaris, tuam deprecantes clementiam: ut in conspectu divinæ majestatis tuæ, pro nostra et totius mundi salute, cum odore suavitatis ascendat. Amen.

IN SPIRITU HUMILITATIS, et in animo contrito suscipiamur a te, Domine: et sic fiat sacrificium nostrum in conspectu tuo hodie, ut placeat tibi, Domine Deus.

VENI, Sanctificator omnipotens æterne Deus: et benedic ✠ hoc sacrificium, tuo sancto nomini præparatum.

PER INTERCESSIONEM beati Michaelis Archangeli, stantis a dextris altaris incensi, et omnium electorum suorum, incensum istud dignetur Dominus benedicere ✠, et in odorem suavitatis accipere. Per Christum Dominum nostrum. Amen.

INCENSUM istud a te benedictum, ascendat ad te, Domine: et descendat super nos misericordia tua.

DIRIGATUR, Domine, oratio mea, sicut incensum in conspectu tuo: elevatio manuum mearum sacrificium vespertinum.

Pone, Domine, custodiam ori meo, et ostium circumstantiæ labiis meis: ut non declinet cor meum in verba malitiæ, ad excusandas excusationes in peccatis.

ACCENDAT in nobis Dominus ignem sui amoris, et flammam æternæ caritatis. Amen.

We offer unto Thee, O Lord, the chalice of salvation, entreating Thy mercy that our offering may ascend with a sweet fragrance in the sight of Thy divine Majesty, for our own salvation, and for that of the whole world. Amen.

Humbled in spirit and contrite of heart, may we find favor with Thee, O Lord: and may our sacrifice be so offered this day in Thy sight as to be pleasing to Thee, O Lord God.

Come Thou, the Sanctifier, Almighty and Everlasting God, and bless ✠ this sacrifice which is prepared for the glory of Thy holy Name.

INCENSING OF THE OFFERINGS AT HIGH MASS

By the intercession of blessed Michael the Archangel, who standeth at the right hand of the Altar of incense, and of all His Elect, may the Lord deign to bless ✠ this incense, and to accept its fragrant sweetness. Through Christ our Lord. Amen.

May this incense which Thou hast blessed, O Lord, ascend to Thee, and may Thy mercy descend upon us.

Welcome as incense-smoke let my prayer rise up before Thee, O Lord. When I lift up my hands, be it as acceptable as the evening sacrifice.

O Lord, set a guard before my mouth, a barrier to fence in my lips. Do not turn my heart toward thoughts of evil, to make excuses for sins.

May the Lord enkindle in us the fire of His love and the flame of everlasting charity. Amen.

LAVABO inter innocentes manus meas: et circumdabo altare tuum, Domine. Ut audiam vocem laudis: et enarrem universa mirabilia tua. Domine, dilexi decorem domus tuæ: et locum habitationis gloriæ tuæ. Ne perdas cum impiis, Deus: animam meam, et cum viris sanguinum vitam meam. In quorum manibus iniquitates sunt: dextera eorum repleta est muneribus.

Ego autem in innocentia mea ingressus sum: redime me, et miserere mei. Pes meus stetit in directo: in ecclesiis benedicam te, Domine.

Gloria Patri, et Filio, et Spiritui Sancto. Sicut erat in principio, et nunc, et semper, et in sæcula sæculorum. Amen.

SUSCIPE, SANCTA TRINITAS, hanc oblationem, quam tibi offerimus ob memoriam passionis, resurrectionis, et ascensionis Jesu Christi Domini nostri, et in honorem beatæ Mariæ semper Virginis, et beati Joannis Baptistæ, et sanctorum Apostolorum Petri et Pauli, et istorum, et omnium Sanctorum: ut illis proficiat ad honorem, nobis autem ad salutem: et illi pro nobis intercedere dignentur in cælis, quorum memoriam agimus in terris. Per eundem Christum Dominum nostrum. Amen.

ORATE, FRATRES: ut meum ac vestrum sacrificium acceptabile fiat apud Deum Patrem omnipotentem.

S. Suscipiat Dominus sacrificium de manibus tuis / ad laudem et gloriam nominis sui, / ad utilitatem quoque nostram, / totiusque Ecclesiæ suæ sanctæ.

P. Amen.

Lavabo—Psalm 25:6-12

I WILL WASH MY HANDS among the innocent, and I will encompass Thine Altar, O Lord. That I may hear the voice of praise, and tell of all Thy wondrous works. I have loved, O Lord, the beauty of Thy house, and the place where Thy glory dwelleth. Take not away my soul, O God, with the wicked, nor my life with men of blood. In whose hands are iniquities, their right hand is filled with gifts.

But as for me, I have walked in my innocence; redeem me, and have mercy on me. My foot hath stood in the right way; in the churches I will bless Thee, O Lord.

Glory be to the Father, and to the Son, and to the Holy Ghost. As it was in the beginning, is now, and ever shall be, world without end. Amen.

Prayer to the Most Holy Trinity

RECEIVE, O HOLY TRINITY, this oblation which we make to Thee in memory of the Passion, Resurrection and Ascension of our Lord Jesus Christ; and in honor of Blessed Mary ever Virgin, of blessed John the Baptist, the holy Apostles Peter and Paul, of these and of all the Saints. To them let it bring honor, and to us salvation, and may they whom we are commemorating here on earth deign to plead for us in heaven. Through the same Christ our Lord. Amen.

Orate Fratres

PRAY, BRETHREN, that my Sacrifice and yours may be acceptable to God the Father Almighty.

S. May the Lord accept the Sacrifice from thy hands, to the praise and glory of His Name, for our benefit and for that of all His holy Church.

P. Amen.

THE SECRET

Suscipe, quæsumus, Domine, pro sacra connubii lege munus oblatum: et, cujus largitor es operis, esto dispositor. Per Dominum nostrum Jesum Christum, Filium tuum, qui tecum vivit et regnat, in unitate Spiritus Sancti, Deus,

P. Per omnia sæcula sæculorum.
S. Amen.
P. Dominus vobiscum.
S. Et cum spiritu tuo.
P. Sursum corda.
S. Habemus ad Dominum.
P. Gratias agamus Domino Deo nostro.
S. Dignum et justum est.

Vere dignum et justum est, æquum et salutare, nos tibi semper et ubique gratias agere: Domine sancte, Pater omnipotens, æterne Deus: per Christum Dominum nostrum. Per quem majestatem tuam laudant Angeli, adorant Dominationes, tremunt Potestates. Cæli, cælorumque Virtutes, ac beata Seraphim, socia exsultatione concelebrant. Cum quibus et nostras voces, ut admitti jubeas, deprecamur, supplici confessione dicentes:

Sanctus, Sanctus, Sanctus, Dominus Deus Sabaoth. Pleni sunt cæli et terra gloria tua. Hosanna in excelsis.

✠ Benedictus qui venit in nomine Domini. Hosanna in excelsis.

THE SECRET (Proper)

Receive, we beseech Thee, O Lord, the offering we make to Thee for the sacred law of matrimony; and be Thou the disposer of the work of which Thou art the author. Through our Lord Jesus Christ Thy Son, Who liveth and reigneth with Thee in the unity of the Holy Ghost, God,

STAND
High Mass

P. World without end.
S. Amen.
P. The Lord be with you.
S. And with thy spirit.
P. Lift up your hearts.
S. We have lifted them up to the Lord.
P. Let us give thanks to the Lord our God.
S. It is right and just.

Preface

IT IS TRULY MEET AND JUST, right and available unto salvation, that we should at all times and in all places, give thanks unto Thee, O holy Lord, Father Almighty, Everlasting God; through Christ our Lord. Through whom the Angels praise Thy majesty, the Dominions worship It, the Powers stand in awe. The heavens, and the heavenly Hosts, and the blessed Seraphim join together in celebrating their joy. With whom we pray Thee join our voices also, while we say with lowly praise:

Sanctus

KNEEL

HOLY, HOLY, HOLY, Lord God of Hosts. Heaven and earth are full of Thy Glory. Hosanna in the highest.

✠ Blessed is He Who cometh in the Name of the Lord. Hosanna in the highest.

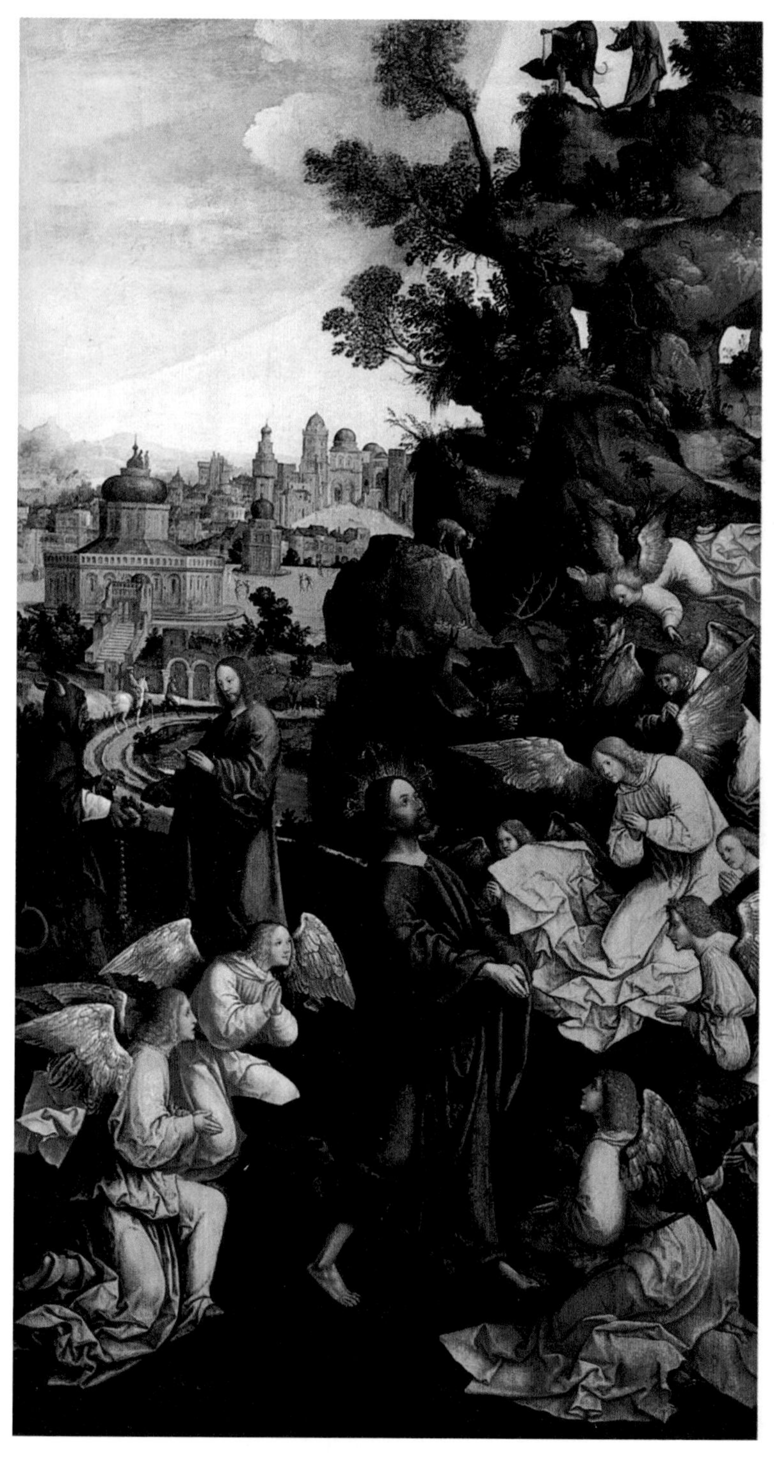

The Temptation of Christ
Jakob Cornelisz

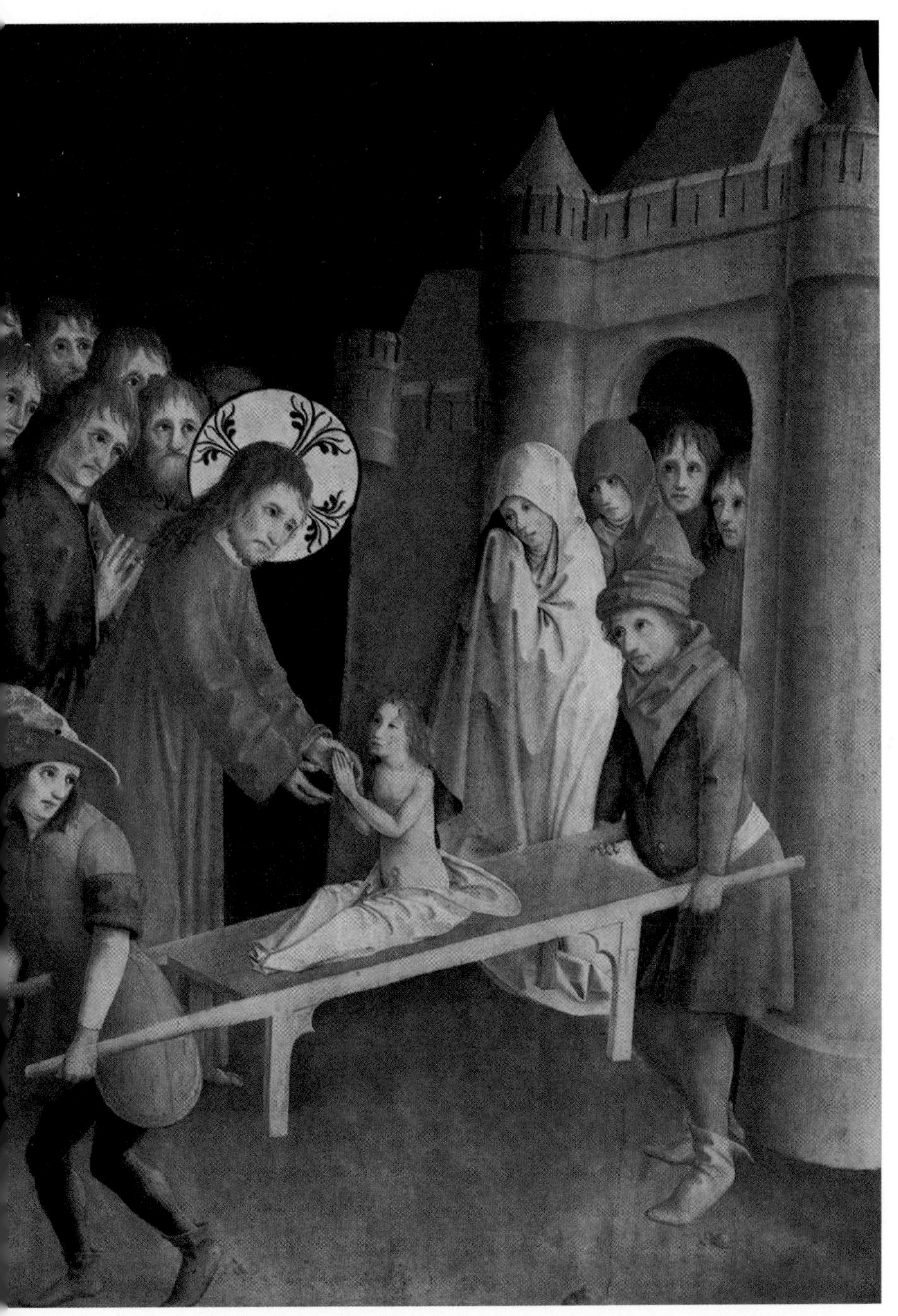

The Healing of the Widow's Son at Nain
The Master of the Darnstadt Passion

Adoration of the Magi Fra Angelico

Nativity
Fra Angelico

Doubting Thomas
Caravaggio

The Annunciation Fra Angelico

Canon

TE IGITUR, clementissime Pater, per Jesum Christum Filium tuum, Dominum nostrum, supplices rogamus, ac petimus, uti accepta habeas, et benedicas, hæc ✠ dona, hæc ✠ munera, hæc ✠ sancta sacrificia illibata, in primis, quæ tibi offerimus pro Ecclesia tua sancta catholica: quam pacificare, custodire, adunare, et regere digneris toto orbe terrarum: una cum famulo tuo Papa nostro N. et Antistite nostro N. et omnibus orthodoxis, atque catholicæ et apostolicæ fidei cultoribus.

MEMENTO, DOMINE, famulorum famularumque tuarum N. et N. et omnium circumstantium, quorum tibi fides cognita est, et nota devotio, pro quibus tibi offerimus: vel qui tibi offerunt hoc sacrificium laudis, pro se, suisque omnibus: pro redemptione animarum suarum, pro spe salutis et incolumitatis suæ: tibique reddunt vota sua æterno Deo, vivo et vero.

Canon

Prayers Before Consecration

FOR THE CHURCH

We, therefore, humbly pray and beseech Thee, most merciful Father, through Jesus Christ Thy Son, our Lord, to accept and to bless these ✠ gifts, these ✠ presents, these ✠ holy unspotted Sacrifices, which we offer up to Thee, in the first place, for Thy Holy Catholic Church, that it may please Thee to grant her peace, to preserve, unite, and govern her throughout the world; as also for Thy servant N. our Pope, and N. our Bishop, and for all orthodox believers and all who profess the Catholic and Apostolic faith.

FOR THE LIVING

Be mindful, O Lord, of Thy servants and handmaids N. and N. and of all here present, whose faith and devotion are known to Thee, for whom we offer, or who offer up to Thee this Sacrifice of praise for themselves and all those dear to them, for the redemption of their souls and the hope of their safety and salvation: who now pay their vows to Thee, the everlasting, living and true God.

Communicantes, et memoriam venerantes, in primis gloriosæ semper Virginis Mariæ, Genitricis Dei et Domini nostri Jesu Christi: sed et beati Joseph ejusdem Virginis Sponsi, et beatorum Apostolorum ac Martyrum tuorum, Petri et Pauli, Andreæ, Jacobi, Joannis, Thomæ, Jacobi, Philippi, Bartholomæi, Matthæi, Simonis et Thaddæi, Lini, Cleti, Clementis, Xysti, Cornelii, Cypriani, Laurentii, Chrysogoni, Joannis et Pauli, Cosmæ et Damiani: et omnium Sanctorum tuorum. Quorum meritis precibusque concedas, ut in omnibus protectionis tuæ muniamur auxilio. Per eundem Christum Dominum nostrum. Amen.

Hanc igitur oblationem servitutis nostræ, sed et cunctæ familiæ tuæ, quæsumus, Domine, ut placatus accipias: diesque nostros in tua pace disponas, atque ab æterna damnatione nos eripi, et in electorum tuorum jubeas grege numerari. Per Christum Dominum nostrum. Amen.

Quam oblationem tu, Deus, in omnibus, quæsumus, bene✠dictam, adscrip✠tam, ra✠tam, rationabilem, acceptabilemque facere digneris: ut nobis Cor✠pus, et San✠guis fiat dilectissimi Filii tui Domini nostri Jesu Christi.

INVOCATION OF THE SAINTS

In communion with, and honoring the memory in the first place of the glorious ever Virgin Mary Mother of our God and Lord Jesus Christ; also of blessed Joseph, her Spouse; and likewise of Thy blessed Apostles and Martyrs, Peter and Paul, Andrew, James, John, Thomas, James, Philip, Bartholomew, Matthew, Simon and Thaddeus, Linus, Cletus, Clement, Sixtus, Cornelius, Cyprian, Lawrence, Chrysogonus, John and Paul, Cosmas and Damian, and of all Thy Saints. Grant for the sake of their merits and prayers that in all things we may be guarded and helped by Thy protection. Through the same Christ our Lord. Amen.

Prayers at Consecration

OBLATION OF THE VICTIM TO GOD

We beseech Thee, O Lord, graciously to accept this oblation of our service and that of Thy whole household. Order our days in Thy peace, and command that we be rescued from eternal damnation and numbered in the flock of Thine elect. Through Christ our Lord. Amen.

Humbly we pray Thee, O God, be pleased to make this same offering wholly blessed, ✠ to consecrate ✠ it and approve ✠ it, making it reasonable and acceptable, so that it may become for us the Body ✠ and Blood ✠ of Thy dearly beloved Son, our Lord Jesus Christ.

QUI PRIDIE quam pateretur, accepit panem in sanctas ac venerabiles manus suas, et elevatis oculis in cælum ad te Deum Patrem suum omnipotentem, tibi gratias agens, bene✠dixit, fregit, deditque discipulis suis, dicens: Accipite, et manducate ex hoc omnes:

HOC EST ENIM CORPUS MEUM.

SIMILI MODO postquam cœnatum est,
accipiens et hunc præclarum Calicem in sanctas ac venerabiles manus suas: item tibi gratias agens, bene✠dixit, deditque discipulis suis, dicens: Accipite, et bibite ex eo omnes:

HIC EST ENIM CALIX SANGUINIS MEI,
NOVI ET ÆTERNI TESTAMENTI:
MYSTERIUM FIDEI:
QUI PRO VOBIS ET PRO MULTIS
EFFUNDETUR IN REMISSIONEM
PECCATORUM.

Hæc quotiescumque feceritis, in mei memoriam facietis.

CONSECRATION OF THE HOST

WHO, the day before He suffered, took bread into His Holy and venerable hands, and having lifted up His eyes to heaven, to Thee, God, His Almighty Father, giving thanks to Thee, blessed it, ✠ broke it, and gave it to His disciples, saying: Take and eat ye all of this:

FOR THIS IS MY BODY.

CONSECRATION OF THE WINE

IN LIKE MANNER, after He had supped, taking also into His holy and venerable hands this goodly chalice, again giving thanks to Thee, He blessed it, ✠ and gave it to His disciples, saying: Take and drink ye all of this:

FOR THIS IS THE CHALICE OF MY BLOOD,

OF THE NEW AND ETERNAL TESTAMENT:

THE MYSTERY OF FAITH:

WHICH SHALL BE SHED FOR YOU

AND FOR MANY

UNTO THE REMISSION OF SINS.

As often as ye shall do these things, ye shall do them in remembrance of Me.

Unde et memores, Domine, nos servi tui, sed et plebs tua sancta, ejusdem Christi Filii tui Domini nostri tam beatæ passionis nec non et ab inferis resurrectionis, sed et in cælos gloriosæ ascensionis: offerimus præclaræ majestati tuæ de tuis donis, ac datis, hostiam ✠ puram, hostiam ✠ sanctam, hostiam ✠ immaculatam, Panem ✠ sanctum vitæ æternæ, et Calicem ✠ salutis perpetuæ.

Supra quæ propitio ac sereno vultu respicere digneris: et accepta habere, sicuti accepta habere dignatus es munera pueri tui justi Abel, et sacrificium Patriarchæ nostri Abrahæ: et quod tibi obtulit summus sacerdos tuus Melchisedech, sanctum sacrificium, immaculatam hostiam.

Supplices te rogamus, omnipotens Deus: jube hæc perferri per manus sancti Angeli tui in sublime altare tuum, in conspectu divinæ majestatis tuæ: ut quotquot ex hac altaris participatione sacrosanctum Filii tui, Cor✠pus, et San✠guinem sumpserimus, omni benedictione cælesti et gratia repleamur. Per eundem Christum Dominum nostrum. Amen.

Memento etiam, Domine, famulorum famularumque tuarum N. et N. qui nos præcesserunt cum signo fidei, et dormiunt in somno pacis. Ipsis, Domine, et omnibus in Christo quiescentibus, locum refrigerii, lucis et pacis, ut indulgeas, deprecamur. Per eundem Christum Dominum nostrum. Amen.

Prayers After Consecration

TO OFFER THE VICTIM

AND NOW, O Lord, we, Thy servants, and with us all Thy holy people, calling to mind the blessed Passion of this same Christ, Thy Son, our Lord, likewise His Resurrection from the grave, and also His glorious Ascension into heaven, do offer unto Thy most sovereign Majesty out of the gifts Thou hast bestowed upon us, a Victim ✠ which is pure, a Victim ✠ which is holy, a Victim ✠ which is spotless, the holy Bread ✠ of life eternal, and the Chalice ✠ of everlasting Salvation.

TO ASK GOD TO ACCEPT OUR OFFERING

DEIGN to look upon them with a favorable and gracious countenance, and to accept them as Thou didst accept the offerings of Thy just servant Abel, and the sacrifice of our Patriarch Abraham, and that which Thy high priest Melchisedech offered up to Thee, a holy Sacrifice, an immaculate Victim.

FOR BLESSINGS

WE HUMBLY beseech Thee, almighty God, to command that these our offerings be carried by the hands of Thy holy Angel to Thine Altar on high, in the sight of Thy divine Majesty, so that those of us who shall receive the most sacred Body ✠ and Blood ✠ of Thy Son by partaking thereof from this Altar may be filled with every grace and heavenly blessing: Through the same Christ our Lord. Amen.

FOR THE DEAD

BE MINDFUL, also, O Lord, of Thy servants and handmaids N. and N. who are gone before us with the sign of faith and who sleep the sleep of peace. To these, O Lord, and to all who rest in Christ, grant, we beseech Thee, a place of refreshment, light and peace. Through the same Christ our Lord. Amen.

Nobis quoque peccatoribus famulis tuis, de multitudine miserationum tuarum sperantibus, partem aliquam, et societatem donare digneris, cum tuis sanctis Apostolis et Martyribus: cum Joanne, Stephano, Matthia, Barnaba, Ignatio, Alexandro, Marcellino, Petro, Felicitate, Perpetua, Agatha, Lucia, Agnete, Cæcilia, Anastasia, et omnibus Sanctis tuis: intra quorum nos consortium, non æstimator meriti, sed veniæ, quæsumus, largitor admitte. Per Christum Dominum nostrum.

Per quem hæc omnia, Domine, semper bona creas, sancti✠ficas, vivi✠ficas, bene✠dicis, et præstas nobis.

Per ip✠sum, et cum ip✠so, et in ip✠so, est tibi Deo Patri ✠ omnipotenti, in unitate Spiritus ✠ Sancti, omnis honor, et gloria.

P. Per omnia sæcula sæculorum.
S. Amen.

Communion

P. Oremus. Præceptis salutaribus moniti, et divina institutione formati, audemus dicere:

Pater noster, qui es in cælis: Sanctificetur nomen tuum: Adveniat regnum tuum: Fiat voluntas tua, sicut in cælo, et in terra. Panem nostrum quotidianum da nobis hodie: Et dimitte nobis debita nostra, sicut et nos dimittimus debitoribus nostris. Et ne nos inducas in tentationem.

S. Sed libera nos a malo.
P. Amen.

FOR ETERNAL HAPPINESS

To us also Thy sinful servants, who put our trust in the multitude of Thy mercies, vouchsafe to grant some part and fellowship with Thy holy Apostles and Martyrs: with John, Stephen, Matthias, Barnabas, Ignatius, Alexander, Marcellinus, Peter, Felicitas, Perpetua, Agatha, Lucy, Agnes, Cecilia, Anastasia, and all Thy Saints. Into their company we beseech Thee admit us, not considering our merits, but freely pardoning our offenses. Through Christ our Lord.

FINAL DOXOLOGY & MINOR ELEVATION

By whom, O Lord, Thou dost always create, sanctify, ✠ quicken, ✠ bless, ✠ and bestow upon us all these good things.

Through Him, ✠ and with Him, ✠ and in Him, ✠ is unto Thee, God the Father ✠ Almighty, in the unity of the Holy ✠ Ghost, all honor and glory.

P. World without end.
S. Amen.

Communion

STAND
High Mass

PATER NOSTER

P. Let us pray. Admonished by Thy saving precepts and following Thy divine instruction, we make bold to say:

Our Father, Who art in heaven, hallowed be Thy Name; Thy kingdom come; Thy will be done on earth as it is in heaven. Give us this day our daily bread; and forgive us our trespasses, as we forgive those who trespass against us. And lead us not into temptation.

S. But deliver us from evil.
P. Amen.

First Prayer

Propitiare Domine, supplicationibus nostris, et institutis tuis, quibus propagationem humani generis ordinasti, benignus assiste: ut, quod te auctore jungitur, te auxiliante servetur. Per Dominum nostrum Jesum Christum, Filium tuum, qui tecum vivit et regnat, in unitate Spiritus Sancti, Deus, per omnia sæcula sæculorum. Amen.

Second Prayer

Deus, qui potestate virtutis tuæ de nihilo cuncta fecisti: qui dispositis universitatis exordiis, homini ad imaginem Dei facto, ideo inseparabile mulieris adjutorium condidisti, ut femineo corpori de virili dares carne principium, docens quod ex uno placuisset, institui, nunquam liceret disjungi: Deus, qui tam excellenti mysterio conjugalem copulam consecrasti, ut Christi et Ecclesiæ sacramentum præsignares in foedere nuptiarum: Deus, per quem mulier jungitur viro, et societas principaliter ordinata, ea benedictione donatur, quæ sola nec per originalis peccati pænam, nec per diluvii est ablata sententiam: respice propitius super hanc famulam tuam, quæ maritali jungenda consortio, tua se expetit protectione muniri: sit in ea jugum dilectionis, et pacis: fidelis et casta nubat in Christo, imitatrixque sanctarum permaneat feminarum: sit amabilis viro suo, ut Rachel: sapiens, ut Rebecca: longæva et fidelis, ut Sara: nihil in ea ex actibus suis ille auctor prævaricationis usurpet: nexa fidei, mandatisque permaneat: uni thoro juncta, contactus illicitos fugiat: muniat infirmitatem suam robore disciplinæ: sit vercundia gravis, pudore venerabilis, doctrinis cælestibus erudita: sit fecunda in sobole, sit probata et innocens: et ad beatorum requiem, atque ad cælestia regna perveniat: et videant ambo filios filiorum suorum, usque in tertiam et quartam generationem, et ad optatam perveniant senectutem. Per Dominum nostrum Jesum Christum, Filium tuum, qui tecum vivit et regnat, in unitate Spiritus Sancti, Deus, per omnia sæcula sæculorum. Amen.

NUPTIAL BLESSING

First Prayer

Be gracious, O Lord, to our humble supplications: and graciously assist this Thine institution, which Thou hast established for the increase of mankind: that what is joined together by Thine authority, may be preserved by Thine aid. Through our Lord Jesus Christ Thy Son, Who liveth and reigneth with Thee in the unity of the Holy Ghost, God, for ever and ever. Amen.

Second Prayer

O God, who by Thine own mighty power, didst make all things out of nothing: who, having set in order the beginnings of the world, didst appoint Woman to be an inseparable helpmate to Man, made like unto God, so that Thou didst give to woman's body its beginnings in man's flesh, thereby teaching that what it pleased Thee to form from one substance, might never be lawfully separated: O God, who, by so excellent a mystery hast consecrated the union of man and wife, as to foreshadow in this nuptial bond the union of Christ with His Church: O God, by whom Woman is joined to Man, and the partnership, ordained from the beginning, is endowed with such blessing that it alone was not withdrawn either by the punishment of original sin, nor by the sentence of the flood: graciously look upon this Thy handmaid, who, about to be joined in wedlock, seeks Thy defense and protection. May it be to her a yoke of love and peace: faithful and chaste, may she be wedded in Christ, and let her ever be the imitator of holy women: let her be dear to husband, like Rachel: wise, like Rebecca: long-lived and faithful, like Sara. Let not the author of deceit work any of his evil deeds in her. May she continue, clinging to the faith and to the commandments. Bound in one union, let her shun all unlawful contact. Let her protect her weakness by the strength of discipline; let her be grave in behavior, respected for modesty, well-instructed in heavenly doctrine. Let her be fruitful in offspring; be approved and innocent; and come to the repose of the blessed and the kingdom of heaven. May they both see their children's children to the third and fourth generation, and may they reach the old age which they desire. Through our Lord Jesus Christ Thy Son, Who liveth and reigneth with Thee in the unity of the Holy Ghost, God, for ever and ever. Amen.

Libera nos, quæsumus, Domine, ab omnibus malis, præteritis, præsentibus, et futuris: et intercedente beata et gloriosa semper Virgine Dei Genitrice Maria, cum beatis Apostolis tuis Petro et Paulo, atque Andrea, et omnibus Sanctis, ✠ da propitius pacem in diebus nostris: ut ope misericordiæ tuæ adjuti, et a peccato simus semper liberi, et ab omni perturbatione securi.

Per eundem Dominum nostrum Jesum Christum Filium tuum, Qui tecum vivit et regnat in unitate Spiritus Sancti Deus,
P. Per omnia sæcula sæculorum.
S. Amen.

P. Pax ✠ Domini sit ✠ semper vobis✠cum.
S. Et cum spiritu tuo.

Hæc commixtio et consecratio Corporis et Sanguinis Domini nostri Jesu Christi, fiat accipientibus nobis in vitam æternam. Amen.

Agnus Dei, qui tollis peccata mundi: miserere nobis.
Agnus Dei, qui tollis peccata mundi: miserere nobis.
Agnus Dei, qui tollis peccata mundi: dona nobis pacem.

Domine Jesu Christe, qui dixisti Apostolis tuis: Pacem relinquo vobis, pacem meam do vobis: ne respicias peccata mea, sed fidem Ecclesiæ tuæ; eamque secundum voluntatem tuam pacificare et coadunare digneris: Qui vivis et regnas Deus per omnia sæcula sæculorum. Amen.

LIBERA NOS

DELIVER US, we beseech Thee, O Lord, from all evils, past, present and to come, and by the intercession of the Blessed and glorious ever Virgin Mary, Mother of God, together with Thy blessed apostles Peter and Paul, and Andrew, and all the Saints, ✠ mercifully grant peace in our days, that through the bounteous help of Thy mercy we may be always free from sin, and safe from all disquiet

BREAKING OF THE HOST

THROUGH the same Jesus Christ, Thy Son our Lord, Who is God living and reigning with Thee in the unity of the Holy Ghost,
P. World without end.
S. Amen.

P. May the peace ✠ of the Lord be ✠ always ✠ with you.
S. And with thy spirit. **KNEEL**

MIXTURE OF THE BODY AND BLOOD

MAY this mingling and hallowing of the Body and Blood of our Lord Jesus Christ be for us who receive it a source of eternal life. Amen.

AGNUS DEI

LAMB OF GOD, Who takest away the sins of the world, have mercy on us.
Lamb of God, Who takest away the sins of the world, have mercy on us.
Lamb of God, Who takest away the sins of the world, grant us peace.

Prayers for Holy Communion

PRAYER FOR PEACE AND FIDELITY

O LORD, Jesus Christ, Who didst say to Thine Apostles: Peace I leave you, My peace I give you: look not upon my sins, but upon the faith of Thy Church; and deign to give her that peace and unity which is agreeable to Thy will: God Who livest and reignest world without end. Amen.

DOMINE Jesu Christe, Fili Dei vivi, qui ex voluntate Patris, cooperante Spiritu Sancto, per mortem tuam mundum vivificasti: libera me per hoc sacrosanctum Corpus et Sanguinem tuum ab omnibus iniquitatibus meis, et universis malis: et fac me tuis semper inhærere mandatis, et a te numquam separari permittas: Qui cum eodem Deo Patre, et Spiritu Sancto vivis et regnas Deus in sæcula sæculorum. Amen.

PERCEPTIO Corporis tui, Domine Jesu Christe, quod ego indignus sumere præsumo, non mihi proveniat in judicium et condemnationem: sed pro tua pietate prosit mihi ad tutamentum mentis et corporis, et ad medelam percipiendam: Qui vivis et regnas cum Deo Patre in unitate Spiritus Sancti Deus, per omnia sæcula sæculorum. Amen.

PANEM cælestem accipiam, et nomen Domini invocabo.

DOMINE, non sum dignus, ut intres sub tectum meum: sed tantum dic verbo, et sanabitur anima mea. (said three times)

CORPUS Domini nostri Jesu Christi custodiat animam meam in vitam æternam. Amen.

QUID retribuam Domino pro omnibus quae retribuit mihi? Calicem salutaris accipiam, et nomen Domini invocabo. Laudans invocabo Dominum, et ab inimicis meis salvus ero.

SANGUIS Domini nostri Jesu Christi custodiat animam meam in vitam æternam. Amen.

PRAYER FOR HOLINESS

O Lord Jesus Christ, Son of the living God, Who, by the will of the Father and the co-operation of the Holy Ghost, hast by Thy death given life to the world: deliver me by this, Thy most sacred Body and Blood, from all my iniquities and from every evil; make me cling always to Thy commandments, and permit me never to be separated from Thee. Who with the same God, the Father and the Holy Ghost, livest and reignest God, world without end. Amen.

PRAYER FOR GRACE

Let not the partaking of Thy Body, O Lord Jesus Christ, which I, though unworthy, presume to receive, turn to my judgment and condemnation; but through Thy mercy may it be unto me a safeguard and a healing remedy both of soul and body. Who livest and reignest with God the Father, in the unity of the Holy Ghost, God, world without end. Amen.

COMMUNION OF THE PRIEST

I will take the Bread of Heaven, and will call upon the name of the Lord.

Lord, I am not worthy that Thou shouldst enter under my roof; but only say the word, and my soul shall be healed. (said three times)

May the Body of our Lord Jesus Christ preserve my soul unto life everlasting. Amen.

What return shall I make to the Lord for all the things that He hath given unto me? I will take the chalice of salvation, and call upon the Name of the Lord. I will call upon the Lord and give praise: and I shall be saved from mine enemies.

May the Blood of our Lord Jesus Christ preserve my soul unto life everlasting. Amen.

ECCE Agnus Dei, ecce qui tollit peccata mundi.

DOMINE, non sum dignus, ut intres sub tectum meum: sed tantum dic verbo, et sanabitur anima mea. (said three times)

CORPUS Domini nostri Jesu Christi custodiat animam tuam in vitam æternam. Amen.

QUOD ore sumpsimus, Domine, pura mente capiamus: et de munere temporali fiat nobis remedium sempiternum.

CORPUS TUUM, Domine, quod sumpsi, et Sanguis, quem potavi, adhæreat visceribus meis: et præsta; ut in me non remaneat scelerum macula, quem pura et sancta refecerunt sacramenta: Qui vivis et regnas in sæcula sæculorum. Amen.

THE COMMUNION VERSE

Ecce sic benedicetur omnis homo, qui timet Dominum: et videas filios filiorum tuorum: pax super Israel. (T.P. Alleluia.)

P. Dominus vobiscum.
S.Et cum spiritu tuo.
P. Oremus.

COMMUNION OF THE FAITHFUL

BEHOLD the Lamb of God, behold Him Who taketh away the sins of the world.

LORD, I am not worthy that Thou shouldst enter under my roof; but only say the word, and my soul shall be healed. (said three times)

MAY the Body of our Lord Jesus Christ preserve your soul unto life everlasting. Amen.

Prayers after Communion

ABLUTIONS

GRANT, O Lord, that what we have taken with our mouth, we may receive with a pure mind; and that from a temporal gift it may become for us an everlasting remedy.

MAY THY BODY, O Lord, which I have received
and Thy Blood which I have drunk, cleave to my
inmost parts, and grant that no stain of sin remain in me; whom these pure and holy Sacraments have refreshed. Who livest and reignest world without
end. Amen.

THE COMMUNION VERSE (Proper)

Behold, thus shall every man be blessed that feareth the Lord; and mayest thou see thy children's children; peace upon Israel. (P.T. Alleluia)

P. The Lord be with you.
S. And with thy spirit.
P. Let us pray.

POSTCOMMUNION

Quæsumus omnipotens Deus, instituta providentiæ tuæ pio favore comitare: ut, quos legitima societate connectis, longæva pace custodias. Per Dominum nostrum Jesum Christum, Filium tuum, qui tecum vivit et regnat, in unitate Spiritus Sancti, Deus, per omnia sæcula sæculorum.
S. Amen.

P. Dominus vobiscum.
S. Et cum spiritu tuo.

P. Ite, Missa est.
S. Deo gratias.

Deus Abraham, Deus Isaac, et Deus Jacob sit vobiscum: et ipse adimpleat benedictionem suam in vobis: ut videatis filios filiorum vestrorum usque ad tertiam et quartam generationem, et postea vitam æternam habeatis sine fine: adjuvante Domino nostro Jesu Christo, qui cum Patre et Spiritu sancto vivit et regnat Deus, per omnia sæcula sæculorum.
S. Amen.

PLACEAT TIBI, sancta Trinitas, obsequium servitutis meæ: et præsta; ut sacrificium, quod oculis tuæ majestatis indignus obtuli, tibi sit acceptabile, mihique, et omnibus, pro quibus illud obtuli, sit, te miserante, propitiabile. Per Christum Dominum nostrum. Amen.

BENEDICAT VOS OMNIPOTENS DEUS, Pater, ✠ et Filius, et Spiritus Sanctus.
S. Amen.

THE POSTCOMMUNION (Proper)

STAND
High Mass

We beseech Thee, almighty God, to accompany the institution of Thy providence with Thy gracious favor; that Thou mayest keep in lasting peace those whom Thou joinest in lawful union. Through our Lord Jesus Christ Thy Son, Who liveth and reigneth with Thee in the unity of the Holy Ghost, God, for ever and ever.
S. Amen.

P. The Lord be with you.
S. And with thy spirit.

THE DISMISSAL

P. Go, the Mass is ended.
S. Thanks be to God.

May the God of Abraham, the God of Isaac, and the God of Jacob be with you, and may He fulfill His blessing in you: that you may see your children's children even to the third and fourth generation, and thereafter may you have life everlasting, by the grace of our Lord Jesus Christ; Who with the Father and the Holy Ghost liveth and reigneth, God for ever and ever.
S. Amen.

THE LAST BLESSING

KNEEL

MAY THE TRIBUTE of my homage be pleasing to Thee, O most holy Trinity. Grant that the Sacrifice which I, unworthy as I am, have offered in the presence of Thy Majesty, may be acceptable to Thee. Through Thy mercy may it bring forgiveness to me and to all for whom I have offered it. Through Christ our Lord. Amen.

MAY ALMIGHTY GOD BLESS YOU: the Father, ✠ the Son, and the Holy Ghost.
S. Amen.

THE LAST GOSPEL (see page 49)

Burial of the Count of Orgaz
El Greco

Requiem Mass

1962 Typical Edition

THE BURIAL SERVICE
MEETING THE BODY

Ant. Si iniquitates observaveris, Domine: Domine, quis sustinebit?

De profundis clamavi ad te, Domine: Domine, exaudi vocem meam.
Fiant aures tuæ intendentes / in vocem deprecationis meæ.
Si iniquitates observaveris, Domine, / Domine, quis sustinebit?
Quia apud te propitiatio est: et propter legem tuam sustinui te, Domine.
Sustinuit anima mea in verbo ejus: speravit anima mea in Domino.
A custodia matutina usque ad noctem: speret Israel in Domino.
Quia apud Dominum misericordia / et copiosa apud eum redemptio.
Et ipse redimet Israel / ex omnibus iniquitatibus ejus.
P. Requiem æternam / dona eis, Domine.
S. Et lux perpetua / luceat eis.
Ant. Si iniquitates observaveris, Domine: Domine, quis sustinebit?

THE BURIAL SERVICE
MEETING THE BODY

STAND

Ant. If Thou, O Lord, wilt mark iniquities, Lord, who shall endure it?

DE PROFUNDIS

Out of the depths I have cried to Thee, O Lord! Lord, hear my voice.
Let Thine ears be attentive to the voice of my supplication.
If Thou, O Lord, shalt observe inquities, O Lord, who shall endure it?
For with Thee there is merciful forgiveness: because of Thy law I wait for Thee, O Lord.
My soul hath relied on His word: my soul hath hoped in the Lord.
From the morning watch even until night, let Israel hope in the Lord:
For with the Lord there is mercy, and with Him is plentiful redemption.
And He shall redeem Israel from all his iniquities.
P. Eternal rest grant unto them, O Lord.
S. And let perpetual light shine upon them.
Ant. If Thou, O Lord, wilt mark iniquities, Lord, who shall endure it?

Ant. Exsultabunt Domino ossa humiliata.

Miserere mei, Deus, / secundum magnam misericordiam tuam.
Et secundum multitudinem miserationum tuarum / dele iniquitatem meam.
Amplius lava me ab iniquitate mea, / et a peccato meo munda me.
Quoniam iniquitatem meam ego cognosco, / et peccatum meum contra me est semper.
Tibi soli peccavi, et malum coram te feci,/ut justificeris in sermonibus tuis, et vincas cum judicaris.
Ecce enim in iniquitatibus conceptus sum, / et in peccatis concepit me mater mea.
Ecce enim veritatem dilexisti: / incerta et occulta sapientiæ tuæ manifestasti mihi.

Asperges me hyssopo, et mundabor: / lavabis me, et super nivem dealbabor.

Auditui meo dabis gaudium et lætitiam, / et exultabunt ossa humiliata.
Averte faciem tuam a peccatis meis, / et omnes iniquitates meas dele.

Cor mundum crea in me, Deus, / et spiritum rectum innova in visceribus meis.
Ne projicias me a facie tua, / et Spiritum sanctum tuum ne auferas a me.
Redde mihi lætitiam salutaris tui, et spiritu principali confirma me.
Docebo iniquos vias tuas, / et impii ad te convertentur.
Libera me de sanguinibus, Deus, Deus salutis meæ: / et exsultabit lingua mea justitiam tuam.

Ant. They shall rejoice in the Lord, the bones that have been humbled.

Have mercy on me, O God, according to Thy great mercy;

And according to the multitude of Thy tender mercies, blot out my iniquity.

Wash me thoroughly from my offense, and cleanse me from my sin.

For I acknowledge mine iniquity, and my sin is always before me.

Against Thee only have I sinned, and I have done that which is evil in Thy sight, that Thou be found just in Thy sentence, upright in Thy judgment.

For, behold, I was born in iniquities, and in sin did my mother conceive me.

For, behold, Thou hast loved truth; the secret and hidden things of Thy wisdom Thou hast made manifest unto me.

Thou shalt sprinkle me with hyssop, and I shall be cleansed; Thou shalt wash me, and I shall become whiter than snow.

Thou shalt make me hear joy and gladness; and the bones that were humbled shall rejoice.

Turn away Thy face from my sins, and blot out all my iniquities.

Create in me a pure heart, O God, and renew a steadfast spirit within me.

Cast me not away from Thy face, and take not Thy Holy Spirit from me.

Restore unto me the joy of Thy salvation, and strengthen me with a noble spirit.

I will teach the unjust Thy ways, and the wicked shall be converted to Thee.

Deliver me from sins of blood, O God, Thou God of my salvation: and my tongue shall extol Thy justice.

Domine, labia mea aperies, / et os meum annuntiabit laudem tuam.
Quoniam si voluisses sacrificium, dedissem utique: / holocaustis non delectaberis.

Sacrificium Deo spiritus contribulatus: / cor contritum et humiliatum, Deus, non despicies.
Benigne fac, Domine, in bona voluntate tua Sion, / ut ædificentur muri Jerusalem.

Tunc acceptabis sacrificium justitiæ, oblationes, et holocausta: / tunc imponent super altare tuum vitulos.
P. Requiem æternam / dona eis, Domine.
S. Et lux perpetua / luceat eis.
Ant. Exsultabunt Domino ossa humiliata.

RESPONSORY: SUBVENITE

Subvenite, / Sancti Dei, occurrite, Angeli Domini; / Suscipientes animam ejus: / Offerentes eam in conspectu Altissimi

P. Suscipiat te Christus, qui vocavit te: et in sinum Abrahæ Angeli deducant te:

S. Suscipientes animam ejus: / Offerentes eam in conspectu Altissimi.
P. Requiem æternam dona ei, Domine: et lux perpetua luceat ei.
S. Offerentes eam in conspectu altissimi.

Thou shalt open my lips, O Lord: and my mouth shall declare Thy praise.
For if Thou hadst desired sacrifice, I would surely have given it: with burnt-offerings Thou wilt not be delighted.
A sacrifice unto God is a troubled spirit: a contrite and humble heart, O God, Thou wilt not despise.
Deal favorably, O Lord, in Thy good will with Sion: that the walls of Jerusalem may be built up.

Then shalt Thou accept the sacrifice of justice, oblations, and whole burnt-offerings: then shall they lay calves upon Thine altar.
P. Eternal rest grant unto them, O Lord.
S. And let perpetual light shine upon them.
Ant. They shall rejoice in the Lord, the bones that have been humbled.

RESPONSORY: SUBVENITE

Come to his (her) assistance, ye saints of God; meet him (her), ye Angels of the Lord, receive his (her) soul, offering it in the sight of the Most High.
P. May Christ, Who has called you, receive you and may the Angels conduct you into Abraham's bosom.
S. Receive his (her) soul, offering it in the sight of the Most High.
P. Eternal rest grant unto him (her), O Lord, and let perpetual light shine upon him (her).
S. Offering it in the sight of the Most High.

THE BURIAL MASS
ON THE DAY OF DEATH OR BURIAL

In nomine Patris, ✠ et Filii, et Spiritus Sancti. Amen.
P. Introibo ad altare Dei.
S. Ad Deum qui lætificat juventutem meam.
P. Adjutorium nostrum ✠ in nomine Domini.
S. Qui fecit cælum et terram.

Confiteor Deo omnipotenti, / beatæ Mariæ semper Virgini, / beato Michaeli Archangelo, / beato Joanni Baptistæ, / Sanctis Apostolis Petro et Paulo, / omnibus sanctis, et vobis fratres / quia peccavi nimis cogitatione, verbo et opere: mea culpa, mea culpa, mea maxima culpa. / Ideo precor beatam Mariam semper Virginem, / beatum Michaelem Archangelum, / beatum Joannem Baptistam, / sanctos Apostolos Petrum et Paulum, / omnes Sanctos, et vos fratres / orare pro me ad Dominum Deum nostrum.

S. Misereatur tui omnipotens Deus, et dimissis peccatis tuis, perducat te ad vitam æternam.

P. Amen.

THE BURIAL MASS
ON THE DAY OF DEATH OR BURIAL

ALL KNEEL **and make the sign of the cross**

In the name of the Father, ✠ and of the Son, and of the Holy Ghost. Amen.
P. I will go in unto the Altar of God.
S. Unto God, Who giveth joy to my youth.
P. Our help ✠ is in the Name of the Lord.
S. Who hath made heaven and earth.

I confess to Almighty God, to blessed Mary ever Virgin, to blessed Michael the Archangel, to blessed John the Baptist, to the holy Apostles Peter and Paul, to all the Saints, and to you, brethren, that I have sinned exceedingly, in thought, word and deed: through my fault, through my fault, through my most grievous fault. Therefore I beseech blessed Mary ever Virgin, blessed Michael the Archangel, blessed John the Baptist, the holy Apostles Peter and Paul, all the Saints, and you, brethren, to pray to the Lord our God for me.

S. May Almighty God have mercy upon you,
forgive you your sins, and bring you to life
everlasting.
P. Amen.

S. Confiteor Deo omnipotenti, / beatæ Mariæ semper Virgini, / beato Michaeli Archangelo, / beato Joanni Baptistæ, / sanctis Apostolis Petro et Paulo, / omnibus Sanctis, et tibi, Pater: / quia peccavi nimis cogitatione, verbo et opere: / mea culpa, mea culpa, mea maxima culpa. / Ideo precor beatam Mariam semper Virginem, / beatum Michaelem Archangelum, / beatum Joannem Baptistam, / sanctos Apostolos Petrum et Paulum, / omnes Sanctos, et te, Pater, / orare pro me ad Dominum Deum nostrum.

P. Misereatur vestri omnipotens Deus, et dimissis peccatis vestris, perducat vos ad vitam æternam.

S. Amen.

P. Indulgentiam, ✠ absolutionem, et remissionem peccatorum nostrorum tribuat nobis omnipotens et misericors Dominus.

S. Amen.

P. Deus, tu conversus vivificabis nos.

S. Et plebs tua lætabitur in te.

P. Ostende nobis, Domine, misericordiam tuam.

S. Et salutare tuum da nobis.

P. Domine, exaudi orationem meam.

S. Et clamor meus ad te veniat.

P. Dominus vobiscum.

S. Et cum spiritu tuo.

P. Oremus.

Aufer a nobis, quæsumus, Domine, iniquitates nostras: ut ad Sancta sanctorum puris mereamur mentibus introire. Per Christum Dominum nostrum. Amen.

S. I confess to Almighty God, to blessed Mary ever Virgin, to blessed Michael the Archangel, to blessed John the Baptist, to the holy Apostles Peter and Paul, to all the Saints, and to you, Father, that I have sinned exceedingly, in thought, word and deed: through my fault, through my fault, through my most grievous fault. Therefore I beseech blessed Mary ever Virgin, blessed Michael the Archangel, blessed John the Baptist, the holy Apostles Peter and Paul, all the Saints, and you, Father, to pray to the Lord our God for me.

P. May Almighty God have mercy upon you, forgive you your sins, and bring you to life everlasting.

S. Amen.

P. May the Almighty and merciful God grant us pardon, ✠ absolution and remission of our sins.

S. Amen.

P. Thou wilt turn, O God, and bring us to life.

S. And Thy people shall rejoice in Thee.

P. Show us, O Lord, Thy mercy.

S. And grant us Thy salvation.

P. O Lord, hear my prayer.

S. And let my cry come unto Thee.

P. The Lord be with you.

S. And with thy spirit.

P. Let us pray.

THE PRIEST ASCENDS THE ALTAR

Take away from us our iniquities, we entreat Thee, O Lord, that with pure minds we may worthily enter into the Holy of Holies. Through Christ our Lord. Amen.

Oramus te, Domine, per merita Sanctorum tuorum, quorum reliquiæ hic sunt, et omnium Sanctorum: ut indulgere digneris omnia peccata mea. Amen.

THE INTROIT

Requiem æternam dona eis, Domine: et lux perpetua luceat eis. Te decet hymnus, Deus, in Sion, et tibi reddetur votum in Jerusalem: exaudi orationem meam, ad te omnis caro veniet.

Requiem æternam dona eis, Domine: et lux perpetua luceat eis.

P. Kyrie, eleison.
S. Kyrie, eleison.
P. Kyrie, eleison.
S. Christe, eleison.
P. Christe, eleison.
S. Christe, eleison.
P. Kyrie, eleison.
S. Kyrie, eleison.
P. Kyrie, eleison.

P. Dominus vobiscum.
S. Et cum spiritu tuo.
P. Oremus.

THE COLLECT

Deus, cui proprium est misereri semper et parcere, te supplices exoramus pro anima famuli tui (famulæ tuæ) N., quam hodie de hoc sæculo migrare jussisti: ut non tradas eam in manus inimici, neque obliviscaris in finem, sed jubeas eam a sanctis Angelis suscipi et ad patriam paradisi perduci; ut,

We beseech Thee, O Lord, by the merits of Thy Saints, whose relics are here, and of all the Saints, that Thou wilt deign to pardon me all my sins. Amen.

THE INTROIT

Eternal rest grant unto them, O Lord; and let perpetual light shine upon them. To Thee is due the hymn, O God, in Sion; and to Thee shall the vow be paid in Jerusalem. Oh, hear my prayer: unto Thee all flesh shall come.
Eternal rest grant unto them, O Lord; and let perpetual light shine upon them.

The Kyrie Eleison

P. Lord, have mercy on us.
S. Lord, have mercy on us.
P. Lord, have mercy on us.
S. Christ, have mercy on us.
P. Christ, have mercy on us.
S. Christ, have mercy on us.
P. Lord, have mercy on us.
S. Lord, have mercy on us.
P. Lord, have mercy on us.

P. The Lord be with you. **STAND**
S. And with thy spirit. **High Mass**
P. Let us pray.

THE COLLECT

O God, Whose property it is always to have mercy and to spare, we humbly entreat Thee for the soul of Thy servant (handmaid) N., whom Thou hast summoned today from this world, that Thou would not deliver him (her) into the hands of the enemy, nor forget him (her) forever, but bid Thy holy Angels receive him (her) and bear him (her) to our

quia in te speravit et credidit, non pœnas inferni sustineat, sed gaudia æterna possideat. Per Dominum nostrum Jesum Christum, Filium tuum, qui tecum vivit et regnat, in unitate Spiritus Sancti, Deus, per omnia sæcula sæculorum.
S. Amen.

THE EPISTLE

Fratres: Nolumus vos ignorare de dormientibus, ut non contristemini, sicut et ceteri, qui spem non habent. Si enim credimus quod Jesus mortuus est, et resurrexit: ita et Deus eos, qui dormierunt per Jesum, adducet cum eo. Hoc enim vobis dicimus in verbo Domini, quia nos, qui vivimus, qui residui sumus in adventum Domini, non præveniemus eos, qui dormierunt. Quoniam ipse Dominus in iussu, et in voce Archangeli, et in tuba Dei descendet de cælo: et mortui, qui in Christo sunt, resurgent primi. Deinde nos, qui vivimus, qui relinquimur, simul rapiemur cum illis in nubibus obviam Christo in aera, et sic semper cum Domino erimus. Itaque consolamini invicem in verbis istis.
S. Deo gratias.

THE GRADUAL

Requiem æternam dona eis, Domine: et lux perpetua luceat eis. — In memoria æterna erit justus: ab auditione mala non timebit.

THE TRACT

Absolve, Domine, animas omnium fidelium defunctorum ab omni vinculo delictorum. — Et gratia tua illis succurrente, mereantur evadere judicium ultionis. — Et lucis æternæ beatitudine perfrui.

home in paradise, so that since he (she) believed and hoped in Thee, he (she) may not undergo the pains of hell but may possess eternal joys. Through our Lord Jesus Christ Thy Son, Who liveth and reigneth with Thee in the unity of the Holy Ghost, God, for ever and ever.
S. Amen.

SIT
High Mass

THE EPISTLE 1 Thessalonians 4:13-18

Brethren: We would not have you ignorant concerning those who are asleep, lest you should grieve, even as others who have no hope. For if we believe that Jesus died and rose again, so with Him God will bring those also who have fallen asleep through Jesus. For this we say to you in the word of the Lord, that we who live, who survive until the coming of the Lord, shall not precede those who have fallen asleep. For the Lord Himself with cry of command, with voice of Archangel, and with trumpet of God, shall descend from heaven, and the dead in Christ will rise up first. Then we who live, who survive, shall be caught up together with them in clouds to meet the Lord in the air, and so we shall ever be with the Lord. Therefore, comfort one another with these words.
S. Thanks be to God.

THE GRADUAL 4 Esdras 2:34, 35; Ps. 111:7

Eternal rest grant to them, O Lord; and let perpetual light shine upon them. — The just man shall be in everlasting remembrance; he shall not be afraid for evil tidings.

THE TRACT

Absolve, O Lord, the souls of the faithful departed from every bond of sin. — And by the help of Thy grace may they be enabled to escape the avenging judgment. — And enjoy the blessedness of light eternal.

SEQUENCE: DIES IRÆ

Dies iræ, dies illa, / Solvet sæclum in favilla: / Teste David cum Sibylla.
Quantus tremor est futurus, / Quando judex est venturus, / Cuncta stricte discussurus!
Tuba, mirum spargens sonum, / Per sepulchra regionum, / Coget omnes ante thronum.
Mors stupebit, et natura, / Cum resurget creatura, / Judicanti responsura.
Liber scriptus proferetur, / In quo totum continetur, / Unde mundus judicetur.
Judex ergo cum sedebit, / Quidquid latet, apparebit: / Nil inultum remanebit.
Quid sum miser tunc dicturus? / Quem patronum rogaturus, / Cum vix justus sit securus?
Rex tremendæ majestatis, / qui salvandos salvas gratis, / Salva me, fons pietatis.
Recordare, Jesu pie, / Quod sum causa tuæ viæ: / Ne me perdas illa die.
Quærens me, sedisti lassus: / Redemisti Crucem passus: / Tantus labor non sit cassus.

Juste judex ultionis, / Donum fac remissionis / Ante diem rationis.
Ingemisco, tamquam reus: / Culpa rubet vultus meus: / Supplicanti parce, Deus.
Qui Mariam absolvisti, / Et latronem exaudisti, / Mihi quoque spem dedisti.
Preces meæ non sunt dignæ: / Sed tu bonus fac benigne, / Ne perenni cremer igne.
Inter oves locum præsta, / Et ab hædis me sequestra, / Statuens in parte dextra.
Confutatis maledictis, / Flammis acribus addictis: / Voca me cum benedictis.
Oro supplex et acclinis, / Cor contritum quasi cinis: / Gere curam mei finis.
Lacrymosa dies illa, / Qua resurget ex favilla / Judicandus homo reus: / Huic ergo parce Deus.
Pie Iesu Domine, dona eis requiem. Amen.

SEQUENCE: DIES IRÆ

Day of wrath, O Day of mourning, Lo, the world in ashes burning—Seer and Sibyl gave the warning.
O what fear man's bosom rendeth, When from heaven the Judge descendeth, On Whose sentence all dependeth!
Wondrous sound the trumpet flingeth, Through earth's sepulchres it ringeth, All before the Throne it bringeth.
Death is struck, and Nature quaking, All creation is awaking—To its Judge an answer making.
Lo, the Book, exactly worded, Wherein all hath been recorded—Thence shall judgment be awarded.
When the Judge His seat attaineth, And each hidden deed arraigneth, Nothing unavenged remaineth.
What shall I, frail man, be pleading? Who for me be interceding, When the just are mercy needing?
King, of majesty tremendous, Who dost free salvation send us, Fount of pity, then befriend us.
Think, kind Jesu, my salvation, Caused Thy wondrous Incarnation—Leave me not to reprobation.
Faint and weary Thou hast sought me, On the Cross of suffering bought me; Shall such grace be vainly brought me?
Righteous Judge of Retribution, Grant Thy gift of absolution, Ere that Reck'ning Day's conclusion.
Guilty, now I pour my moaning, All my shame with anguish owning: Spare, O God, Thy suppliant groaning.
Thou the sinful Mary savest, Thou the dying thief forgavest, And to me a hope vouchsafest.
Worthless are my prayers and sighing, Yet, good Lord, in grace complying, Rescue me from fires undying.
With Thy favored sheep O place me; Nor among the goats abase me, But to Thy Right Hand upraise me.
While the wicked are confounded, Doomed to flames of woe unbounded, Call me with Thy saints surrounded.
Low I kneel, with heart's submission; See, like ashes, my contrition—Help me in my last condition.
Ah, that day of tears and mourning, From the dust of earth returning, Man for Judgment must prepare him,
Spare, O God, in mercy spare him. Lord, who didst our souls redeem, Grant a blessed Requiem. Amen

Munda cor meum ac labia mea, omnipotens Deus, qui labia Isaiæ Prophetæ calculo mundasti ignito: ita me tua grata miseratione dignare mundare, ut sanctum Evangelium tuum digne valeam nuntiare. Per Christum Dominum nostrum. Amen.

Jube, Domine, benedicere.

Dominus sit in corde meo, et in labiis meis: ut digne et competenter annuntiem Evangelium suum. Amen.

THE GOSPEL

P. Dominus vobiscum.

S. Et cum spiritu tuo.

P. ✠ Sequentia sancti Evangelii secundum Joannem.

S. Gloria tibi, Domine.

In illo tempore: Dixit Martha ad Jesum: Domine, si fuisses hic, frater meus non fuisset mortuus: sed et nunc scio, quia quæcumque poposceris a Deo, dabit tibi Deus. Dicit illi Jesus: Resurget frater tuus. Dicit ei Martha: Scio quia resurget in resurrectione in novissimo die. Dixit ei Jesu: Ego sum resurrectio, et vita: qui credit in me, etiam si mortuus fuerit, vivet: et omnis qui vivit, et credit in me, non morietur in æternum. Credis hoc? Ait illi: Utique, Domine, ego credidi, quia tu es Christus Filius Dei vivi, qui in hunc mundum venisti.

SERMON (NO CREED)

P. Dominus vobiscum.

S. Et cum spiritu tuo.

P. Oremus.

MUNDA COR MEUM

Cleanse my heart and my lips, O Almighty God, Who didst cleanse the lips of the prophet Isaias with a burning coal; through Thy gracious mercy so purify me that I may worthily proclaim Thy holy Gospel. Through Christ our Lord. Amen.

Grant, O Lord, Thy blessing.

May the Lord be in my heart and on my lips that I may worthily and fittingly proclaim His Gospel. Amen.

THE GOSPEL John 11: 21-27

STAND

P. The Lord be with you.

S. And with thy spirit.

P. ✠ The continuation of the holy Gospel according to St. John.

S. Glory be to Thee, O Lord.

At that time Martha said to Jesus: "Lord, if Thou hadst been here, my brother would not have died. But even now I know that whatever Thou wilt ask of God, God will give it to Thee." Jesus said to her: "Thy brother shall rise." Martha said to Him: "I know that he will rise at the resurrection at the last day." Jesus said to her: "I am the Resurrection and the Life; he who believes in Me, even if he die, shall live; and whoever lives and believes in Me, shall never die. Dost thou believe this?" She said to Him: "Yes, Lord, I believe that Thou art the Christ the Son of the living God, Who art come into this world."

SERMON (NO CREED)

P. The Lord be with you.

S. And with your spirit.

P. Let us pray.

SIT

STAND

THE OFFERTORY

Domine Jesu Christe, Rex gloriæ, libera animas omnium fidelium defunctorum de pœnis inferni et de profundo lacu: libera eas de ore leonis, ne absorbeat eas tartarus, ne cadant in obscurum: sed signifer sanctus Michaël repræsentet eas in lucem sanctam: Quam olim Abrahæ promisisti, et semini ejus. Hostias et preces tibi, Domine, laudis offerimus: tu suscipe pro animabus illis, quarum hodie memoriam facimus: fac eas, Domine, de morte transire ad vitam: Quam olim Abrahæ promisisti, et semini ejus.

Suscipe, sancte Pater, omnipotens æterne Deus, hanc immaculatam hostiam, quam ego indignus famulus tuus offero tibi Deo meo vivo et vero, pro innumerabilibus peccatis, et offensionibus, et negligentiis meis, et pro omnibus circumstantibus, sed et pro omnibus fidelibus christianis vivis atque defunctis: ut mihi et illis proficiat ad salutem in vitam æternam. Amen.

Deus, ✠ qui humanæ substantiæ dignitatem mirabiliter condidisti et mirabilius reformasti: da nobis, per hujus aquæ et vini mysterium, ejus divinitatis esse consortes, qui humanitatis nostræ fieri dignatus est particeps, Jesus Christus, Filius tuus, Dominus noster: Qui tecum vivit et regnat in unitate Spiritus Sancti Deus: per omnia sæcula sæculorum. Amen.

THE OFFERTORY

SIT

O Lord Jesus Christ, King of glory, deliver the souls of all the faithful departed from the pains of hell and from the deep pit: deliver them from the lion's mouth, that hell may not swallow them up, and may they not fall into darkness; but may the holy standard-bearer, Michael, lead them into the holy Light; Which Thou promised to Abraham and to his seed of old. We offer to Thee, Lord, sacrifices and prayers; do Thou receive them in behalf of those souls whom we commemorate this day. Grant them, O Lord, to pass from death to that life; Which Thou promised to Abraham and to his seed of old.

Offering of the Bread and Wine

Accept, O Holy Father, Almighty and Everlasting God, this unspotted Host, which I, Thine unworthy servant, offer unto Thee, my living and true God, to atone for my countless sins, offenses, and negligences: on behalf of all here present and likewise for all faithful Christians, living and dead, that it may avail both me and them as a means of salvation, unto life everlasting. Amen.

O God, ✠ Who in creating man didst exalt his nature very wonderfully and yet more wonderfully didst establish it anew; by the Mystery signified in the mingling of this water and wine, grant us to have part in the Godhead of Him Who hath deigned to become a partaker of our humanity, Jesus Christ, Thy Son, our Lord; Who liveth and reigneth with Thee, in the unity of the Holy Ghost, God. World without end. Amen.

Offerimus tibi, Domine, calicem salutaris, tuam deprecantes clementiam: ut in conspectu divinæ majestatis tuæ, pro nostra et totius mundi salute, cum odore suavitatis ascendat. Amen.

In spiritu humilitatis, et in animo contrito suscipiamur a te, Domine: et sic fiat sacrificium nostrum in conspectu tuo hodie, ut placeat tibi, Domine Deus.

Veni, Sanctificator omnipotens æterne Deus: et benedic ✠ hoc sacrificium, tuo sancto nomini præparatum.

Per intercessionem beati Michaelis Archangeli, stantis a dextris altaris incensi, et omnium electorum suorum, incensum istud dignetur Dominus benedicere ✠, et in odorem suavitatis accipere. Per Christum Dominum nostrum. Amen.

Incensum istud a te benedictum, ascendat ad te, Domine: et descendat super nos misericordia tua.

Dirigatur, Domine, oratio mea, sicut incensum in conspectu tuo: elevatio manuum mearum sacrificium vespertinum.

Pone, Domine, custodiam ori meo, et ostium circumstantiæ labiis meis: ut non declinet cor meum in verba malitiæ, ad excusandas excusationes in peccatis.

Accendat in nobis Dominus ignem sui amoris, et flammam æternæ caritatis. Amen.

We offer unto Thee, O Lord, the chalice of salvation, entreating Thy mercy that our offering may ascend with a sweet fragrance in the sight of Thy divine Majesty, for our own salvation, and for that of the whole world. Amen.

Humbled in spirit and contrite of heart, may we find favor with Thee, O Lord: and may our sacrifice be so offered this day in Thy sight as to be pleasing to Thee, O Lord God.

Come Thou, the Sanctifier, Almighty and Everlasting God, and bless ✠ this sacrifice which is prepared for the glory of Thy holy Name.

INCENSING OF THE OFFERINGS AT HIGH MASS

By the intercession of blessed Michael the Archangel, who standeth at the right hand of the Altar of incense, and of all His Elect, may the Lord deign to bless ✠ this incense, and to accept its fragrant sweetness. Through Christ our Lord. Amen.

May this incense which Thou hast blessed, O Lord, ascend to Thee, and may Thy mercy descend upon us.

Welcome as incense-smoke let my prayer rise up before Thee, O Lord. When I lift up my hands, be it as acceptable as the evening sacrifice.

O Lord, set a guard before my mouth, a barrier to fence in my lips. Do not turn my heart toward thoughts of evil, to make excuses for sins.

May the Lord enkindle in us the fire of His love and the flame of everlasting charity. Amen.

Lavabo inter innocentes manus meas: et circumdabo altare tuum, Domine. Ut audiam vocem laudis: et enarrem universa mirabilia tua. Domine, dilexi decorem domus tuæ: et locum habitationis gloriæ tuæ. Ne perdas cum impiis, Deus: animam meam, et cum viris sanguinum vitam meam. In quorum manibus iniquitates sunt: dextera eorum repleta est muneribus.

Ego autem in innocentia mea ingressus sum: redime me, et miserere mei. Pes meus stetit in directo: in ecclesiis benedicam te, Domine.

Suscipe, sancta Trinitas, hanc oblationem, quam tibi offerimus ob memoriam passionis, resurrectionis, et ascensionis Jesu Christi Domini nostri, et in honorem beatæ Mariæ semper Virginis, et beati Joannis Baptistæ, et sanctorum Apostolorum Petri et Pauli, et istorum, et omnium Sanctorum: ut illis proficiat ad honorem, nobis autem ad salutem: et illi pro nobis intercedere dignentur in cælis, quorum memoriam agimus in terris. Per eundem Christum Dominum nostrum. Amen.

Orate, fratres: ut meum ac vestrum sacrificium acceptabile fiat apud Deum Patrem omnipotentem.

S. Suscipiat Dominus sacrificium de manibus tuis / ad laudem et gloriam nominis sui, / ad utilitatem quoque nostram, / totiusque Ecclesiæ suæ sanctæ.

P. Amen.

THE SECRET

Propitiare quæsumus, Domine, animæ famuli tui (famulæ tuæ) N., pro qua hostiam laudis tibi

LAVABO—PSALM 25:6-12

I will wash my hands among the innocent, and I will encompass Thine Altar, O Lord. That I may hear the voice of praise, and tell of all Thy wondrous works. I have loved, O Lord, the beauty of Thy house, and the place where Thy glory dwelleth. Take not away my soul, O God, with the wicked, nor my life with men of blood. In whose hands are iniquities, their right hand is filled with gifts.

But as for me, I have walked in my innocence; redeem me, and have mercy on me. My foot hath stood in the right way; in the churches I will bless Thee, O Lord.

PRAYER TO THE MOST HOLY TRINITY

Receive, O Holy Trinity, this oblation which we make to Thee in memory of the Passion, Resurrection and Ascension of our Lord Jesus Christ; and in honor of Blessed Mary ever Virgin, of blessed John the Baptist, the holy Apostles Peter and Paul, of these and of all the Saints. To them let it bring honor, and to us salvation, and may they whom we are commemorating here on earth deign to plead for us in heaven. Through the same Christ our Lord. Amen.

ORATE FRATRES

Pray, brethren, that my Sacrifice and yours may be acceptable to God the Father Almighty.

S. May the Lord accept the Sacrifice from thy hands, to the praise and glory of His Name, for our benefit and for that of all His holy Church.

P. Amen.

THE SECRET

Have pity, we pray Thee, Lord, on the soul of Thy servant (handmaid) N., for whom we offer this

immolamus, majestatem tuam suppliciter deprecantes: ut, per hæc piæ placationis officia, pervenire mereatur ad requiem sempiternam. Per Dominum nostrum Jesum Christum, Filium tuum, qui tecum vivit et regnat, in unitate Spiritus Sancti, Deus,

P. Per omnia sæcula sæculorum.
S. Amen.
P. Dominus vobiscum.
S. Et cum spiritu tuo.
P. Sursum corda.
S. Habemus ad Dominum.
P. Gratias agamus Domino Deo nostro.
S. Dignum et justum est.

Vere dignum et justum est, æquum et salutare, nos tibi semper et ubique gratias agere: Domine sancte, Pater omnipotens, æterne Deus: per Christum Dominum nostrum. In quo nobis spes beatæ resurrectionis effulsit, ut quos contristat certa moriendi conditio, eosdem consoletur futuræ immortalitatis promissio. Tuis enim fidelibus, Domine, vita mutatur, non tollitur, et dissoluta terrestris hujus incolatus domo, æterna in cælis habitatio comparatur. Et ideo cum Angelis et Archangelis, cum Thronis et Dominationibus, cumque omni militia cælestis exercitus, hymnum gloriæ tuæ canimus, sine fine dicentes:

Sanctus, Sanctus, Sanctus, Dominus Deus Sabaoth. Pleni sunt cæli et terra gloria tua. Hosanna in excelsis.

✠ Benedictus qui venit in nomine Domini. Hosanna in excelsis.

sacrifice of praise, humbly entreating Thy Majesty that through our holy offering of expiation he (she) may attain to eternal rest. Through our Lord Jesus Christ Thy Son, Who liveth and reigneth with Thee in the unity of the Holy Ghost, God,

STAND
High Mass

P. World without end.
S. Amen.
P. The Lord be with you.
S. And with thy spirit.
P. Lift up your hearts.
S. We have lifted them up to the Lord.
P. Let us give thanks to the Lord our God.
S. It is right and just.

PREFACE

It is truly meet and just, right and proper and for our welfare, that we should always and everywhere give thanks to Thee, Holy Lord, Almighty Father, eternal God, through Christ our Lord. In Him there has dawned for us the hope of a blessed resurrection, heartening with a promise of immortality to come those of us who are saddened by the certainty of dying. The life of those who are faithful to Thee, O Lord, is but changed, not ended; and when their earthly dwelling-place decays, an everlasting mansion stands prepared for them in heaven. Therefore it is that with Angels and Archangels, Thrones and Dominations, and all the warriors of the heavenly array, we chant an endless hymn in praise of Thee, singing:

SANCTUS

Holy, Holy, Holy, Lord God of Hosts. Heaven and earth are full of Thy Glory. Hosanna in the highest.

KNEEL

✠ Blessed is He Who cometh in the Name of the Lord. Hosanna in the highest.

CANON

Te igitur, clementissime Pater, per Jesum Christum Filium tuum, Dominum nostrum, supplices rogamus, ac petimus, uti accepta habeas, et benedicas, hæc ✠ dona, hæc ✠ munera, hæc ✠ sancta sacrificia illibata, in primis, quæ tibi offerimus pro Ecclesia tua sancta catholica: quam pacificare, custodire, adunare, et regere digneris toto orbe terrarum: una cum famulo tuo Papa nostro N. et Antistite nostro N. et omnibus orthodoxis, atque catholicæ et apostolicæ fidei cultoribus.

Memento, Domine, famulorum famularumque tuarum N. et N. et omnium circumstantium, quorum tibi fides cognita est, et nota devotio, pro quibus tibi offerimus: vel qui tibi offerunt hoc sacrificium laudis, pro se, suisque omnibus: pro redemptione animarum suarum, pro spe salutis et incolumitatis suæ: tibique reddunt vota sua æterno Deo, vivo et vero.

CANON

Prayers Before Consecration

FOR THE CHURCH

We, therefore, humbly pray and beseech Thee, most merciful Father, through Jesus Christ Thy Son, Our Lord, to accept and to bless these ✠ gifts, these ✠ presents, these ✠ holy unspotted Sacrifices, which we offer up to Thee, in the first place, for Thy Holy Catholic Church, that it may please Thee to grant her peace, to preserve, unite, and govern her throughout the world; as also for Thy servant N. our Pope, and N. our Bishop, and for all orthodox believers and all who profess the Catholic and Apostolic faith.

FOR THE LIVING

Be mindful, O Lord, of Thy servants and handmaids N. and N. and of all here present, whose faith and devotion are known to Thee, for whom we offer, or who offer up to Thee this Sacrifice of praise for themselves and all those dear to them, for the redemption of their souls and the hope of their safety and salvation: who now pay their vows to Thee, the everlasting, living and true God.

Communicantes, et memoriam venerantes, in primis gloriosæ semper Virginis Mariæ, Genitricis Dei et Domini nostri Jesu Christi: sed et beati Joseph ejusdem Virginis Sponsi, et beatorum Apostolorum ac Martyrum tuorum, Petri et Pauli, Andreæ, Jacobi, Joannis, Thomæ, Jacobi, Philippi, Bartholomæi, Matthæi, Simonis et Thaddæi: Lini, Cleti, Clementis, Xysti, Cornelii, Cypriani, Laurentii, Chrysogoni, Joannis et Pauli, Cosmæ et Damiani: et omnium Sanctorum tuorum; quorum meritis precibusque concedas, ut in omnibus protectionis tuæ muniamur auxilio. Per eundem Christum Dominum nostrum. Amen.

Hanc igitur oblationem servitutis nostræ, sed et cunctæ familiæ tuæ, quæsumus, Domine, ut placatus accipias: diesque nostros in tua pace disponas, atque ab æterna damnatione nos eripi, et in electorum tuorum jubeas grege numerari. Per Christum Dominum nostrum. Amen.

Quam oblationem tu, Deus, in omnibus, quæsumus, bene✠dictam, adscrip✠tam, ra✠tam, rationabilem, acceptabilemque facere digneris: ut nobis Cor✠pus, et San✠guis fiat dilectissimi Filii tui Domini nostri Jesu Christi.

INVOCATION OF THE SAINTS

In communion with, and honoring the memory in the first place of the glorious ever Virgin Mary Mother of our God and Lord Jesus Christ; also of blessed Joseph, her Spouse; and likewise of Thy blessed Apostles and Martyrs, Peter and Paul, Andrew, James, John, Thomas, James, Philip, Bartholomew, Matthew, Simon and Thaddeus, Linus, Cletus, Clement, Sixtus, Cornelius, Cyprian, Lawrence, Chrysogonus, John and Paul, Cosmas and Damian, and of all Thy Saints. Grant for the sake of their merits and prayers that in all things we may be guarded and helped by Thy protection. Through the same Christ our Lord. Amen.

Prayers at Consecration

OBLATION OF THE VICTIM TO GOD

We beseech Thee, O Lord, graciously to accept this oblation of our service and that of Thy whole household. Order our days in Thy peace, and command that we be rescued from eternal damnation and numbered in the flock of Thine elect. Through Christ our Lord. Amen.

Humbly we pray Thee, O God, be pleased to make this same offering wholly blessed, ✠ to consecrate ✠ it and approve ✠ it, making it reasonable and acceptable, so that it may become for us the Body ✠ and Blood ✠ of Thy dearly beloved Son, our Lord Jesus Christ.

Qui pridie quam pateretur, accepit panem in sanctas ac venerabiles manus suas, et elevatis oculis in cælum ad te Deum Patrem suum omnipotentem, tibi gratias agens, bene✠dixit, fregit, deditque discipulis suis, dicens: Accipite, et manducate ex hoc omnes:

HOC EST ENIM CORPUS MEUM.

Simili modo postquam cœnatum est,
accipiens et hunc præclarum Calicem in sanctas ac venerabiles manus suas: item tibi gratias agens, bene✠dixit, deditque discipulis suis, dicens: Accipite, et bibite ex eo omnes:

HIC EST ENIM CALIX SANGUINIS MEI,

NOVI ET ÆTERNI TESTAMENTI:

MYSTERIUM FIDEI:

QUI PRO VOBIS ET PRO MULTIS

EFFUNDETUR IN REMISSIONEM

PECCATORUM.

Hæc quotiescumque feceritis, in mei memoriam facietis.

CONSECRATION OF THE HOST

Who, the day before He suffered, took bread into His Holy and venerable hands, and having lifted up His eyes to heaven, to Thee, God, His Almighty Father, giving thanks to Thee, blessed it, ✠ broke it, and gave it to His disciples, saying: Take and eat ye all of this:

FOR THIS IS MY BODY.

CONSECRATION OF THE WINE

In like manner, after He had supped, taking also into His holy and venerable hands this goodly chalice, again giving thanks to Thee, He blessed it, ✠ and gave it to His disciples, saying: Take and drink ye all of this:

FOR THIS IS THE CHALICE OF MY BLOOD,

OF THE NEW AND ETERNAL TESTAMENT:

THE MYSTERY OF FAITH:

WHICH SHALL BE SHED FOR YOU

AND FOR MANY

UNTO THE REMISSION OF SINS.

As often as ye shall do these things, ye shall do them in remembrance of Me.

Unde et memores, Domine, nos servi tui, sed et plebs tua sancta, ejusdem Christi Filii tui Domini nostri tam beatæ passionis nec non et ab inferis resurrectionis, sed et in cælos gloriosæ ascensionis: offerimus præclaræ majestati tuæ de tuis donis, ac datis, hostiam ✠ puram, hostiam ✠ sanctam, hostiam ✠ immaculatam, Panem ✠ sanctum vitæ æternæ, et Calicem ✠ salutis perpetuæ.

Supra quæ propitio ac sereno vultu respicere digneris: et accepta habere, sicuti accepta habere dignatus es munera pueri tui justi Abel, et sacrificium Patriarchæ nostri Abrahæ: et quod tibi obtulit summus sacerdos tuus Melchisedech, sanctum sacrificium, immaculatam hostiam.

Supplices te rogamus, omnipotens Deus: jube hæc perferri per manus sancti Angeli tui in sublime altare tuum, in conspectu divinæ majestatis tuæ: ut quotquot ex hac altaris participatione sacrosanctum Filii tui, Cor✠pus, et San✠guinem sumpserimus, omni benedictione cælesti et gratia repleamur. Per eundem Christum Dominum nostrum. Amen.

Memento etiam, Domine, famulorum famularumque tuarum N. et N. qui nos præcesserunt cum signo fidei, et dormiunt in somno pacis. Ipsis, Domine, et omnibus in Christo quiescentibus, locum refrigerii, lucis et pacis, ut indulgeas, deprecamur. Per eundem Christum Dominum nostrum. Amen.

Prayers After Consecration

TO OFFER THE VICTIM

And now, O Lord, we, Thy servants, and with us all Thy holy people, calling to mind the blessed Passion of this same Christ, Thy Son, our Lord, likewise His Resurrection from the grave, and also His glorious Ascension into heaven, do offer unto Thy most sovereign Majesty out of the gifts Thou hast bestowed upon us, a Victim ✠ which is pure, a Victim ✠ which is holy, a Victim ✠ which is spotless, the holy Bread ✠ of life eternal, and the Chalice ✠ of everlasting Salvation.

TO ASK GOD TO ACCEPT OUR OFFERING

Deign to look upon them with a favorable and gracious countenance, and to accept them as Thou didst accept the offerings of Thy just servant Abel, and the sacrifice of our Patriarch Abraham, and that which Thy high priest Melchisedech offered up to Thee, a holy Sacrifice, an immaculate Victim.

FOR BLESSINGS

We humbly beseech Thee, almighty God, to command that these our offerings be carried by the hands of Thy holy Angel to Thine Altar on high, in the sight of Thy divine Majesty, so that those of us who shall receive the most sacred Body ✠ and Blood ✠ of Thy Son by partaking thereof from this Altar may be filled with every grace and heavenly blessing: Through the same Christ our Lord. Amen.

FOR THE DEAD

Be mindful, also, O Lord, of Thy servants and handmaids N. and N. who are gone before us with the sign of faith and who sleep the sleep of peace. To these, O Lord, and to all who rest in Christ, grant, we beseech Thee, a place of refreshment, light and peace. Through the same Christ our Lord. Amen.

Nobis quoque peccatoribus famulis tuis, de multitudine miserationum tuarum sperantibus, partem aliquam, et societatem donare digneris, cum tuis sanctis Apostolis et Martyribus: cum Joanne, Stephano, Matthia, Barnaba, Ignatio, Alexandro, Marcellino, Petro, Felicitate, Perpetua, Agatha, Lucia, Agnete, Cæcilia, Anastasia, et omnibus Sanctis tuis: intra quorum nos consortium, non æstimator meriti, sed veniæ, quæsumus, largitor admitte. Per Christum Dominum nostrum.

Per quem hæc omnia, Domine, semper bona creas, sancti✠ficas, vivi✠ficas, bene✠dicis, et præstas nobis.

Per ip✠sum, et cum ip✠so, et in ip✠so, est tibi Deo Patri ✠ omnipotenti, in unitate Spiritus ✠ Sancti, omnis honor, et gloria.
P. Per omnia sæcula sæculorum.
S. Amen.

COMMUNION

P. Oremus.
Præceptis salutaribus moniti, et divina institutione formati, audemus dicere:

Pater noster, qui es in cælis: Sanctificetur nomen tuum: Adveniat regnum tuum: Fiat voluntas tua, sicut in cælo, et in terra. Panem nostrum quotidianum da nobis hodie: Et dimitte nobis debita nostra, sicut et nos dimittimus debitoribus nostris. Et ne nos inducas in tentationem.
S. Sed libera nos a malo.
P. Amen.

FOR ETERNAL HAPPINESS

To us also Thy sinful servants, who put our trust in the multitude of Thy mercies, vouchsafe to grant some part and fellowship with Thy holy Apostles and Martyrs: with John, Stephen, Matthias, Barnabas, Ignatius, Alexander, Marcellinus, Peter, Felicitas, Perpetua, Agatha, Lucy, Agnes, Cecilia, Anastasia, and all Thy Saints. Into their company we beseech Thee admit us, not considering our merits, but freely pardoning our offenses. Through Christ our Lord.

FINAL DOXOLOGY & MINOR ELEVATION

By whom, O Lord, Thou dost always create, sanctify, ✠ quicken, ✠ bless, ✠ and bestow upon us all these good things.

Through Him, ✠ and with Him, ✠ and in Him, ✠ is unto Thee, God the Father ✠ Almighty, in the unity of the Holy ✠ Ghost, all honor and glory.
P. World without end.
S. Amen.

STAND
High Mass

COMMUNION

PATER NOSTER

P. Let us pray. Admonished by Thy saving precepts and following Thy divine instruction, we make bold to say:

Our Father, Who art in heaven, hallowed be Thy Name; Thy kingdom come; Thy will be done on earth as it is in heaven. Give us this day our daily bread; and forgive us our trespasses, as we forgive those who trespass against us. And lead us not into temptation.
S. But deliver us from evil.
P. Amen.

Libera nos, quæsumus, Domine, ab omnibus malis, præteritis, præsentibus, et futuris: et intercedente beata et gloriosa semper Virgine Dei Genitrice Maria, cum beatis Apostolis tuis Petro et Paulo, atque Andrea, et omnibus Sanctis, ✠ da propitius pacem in diebus nostris: ut ope misericordiæ tuæ adjuti, et a peccato simus semper liberi, et ab omni perturbatione securi.

Per eundem Dominum nostrum Jesum Christum Filium tuum,
Qui tecum vivit et regnat in unitate Spiritus Sancti Deus,
P. Per omnia sæcula sæculorum.
S. Amen.

P. Pax ✠ Domini sit ✠ semper vobis✠cum.
S. Et cum spiritu tuo.

Hæc commixtio et consecratio Corporis et Sanguinis Domini nostri Jesu Christi, fiat accipientibus nobis in vitam æternam. Amen.

Agnus Dei, qui tollis peccata mundi: Dona eis requiem.
Agnus Dei, qui tollis peccata mundi: Dona eis requiem.
Agnus Dei, qui tollis peccata mundi: Dona eis requiem sempiternam.

Domine Jesu Christe, Fili Dei vivi, qui ex voluntate Patris, cooperante Spiritu Sancto, per mortem tuam mundum vivificasti: libera me

LIBERA NOS

Deliver us, we beseech Thee, O Lord, from all evils, past, present and to come, and by the intercession of the Blessed and glorious ever Virgin Mary, Mother of God, together with Thy blessed apostles Peter and Paul, and Andrew, and all the Saints, ✠ mercifully grant peace in our days, that through the bounteous help of Thy mercy we may be always free from sin, and safe from all disquiet.

BREAKING OF THE HOST

Through the same Jesus Christ, Thy Son our Lord, Who is God living and reigning with Thee in the unity of the Holy Ghost,

P. World without end.
S. Amen.

P. May the peace ✠ of the Lord be ✠ always ✠ with you.
S. And with thy spirit.

KNEEL

MIXTURE OF THE BODY AND BLOOD

May this mingling and hallowing of the Body and Blood of our Lord Jesus Christ be for us who receive it a source of eternal life. Amen.

AGNUS DEI

Lamb of God, Who takest away the sins of the world, grant them rest.
Lamb of God, Who takest away the sins of the world, grant them rest.
Lamb of God, Who takest away the sins of the world, grant them eternal rest.

Prayers for Holy Communion

PRAYER FOR HOLINESS

O Lord Jesus Christ, Son of the living God, Who, by the will of the Father and the co-operation of the Holy Ghost, hast by Thy death given

per hoc sacrosanctum Corpus et Sanguinem tuum ab omnibus iniquitatibus meis, et universis malis: et fac me tuis semper inhærere mandatis, et a te numquam separari permittas: Qui cum eodem Deo Patre, et Spiritu Sancto vivis et regnas Deus in sæcula sæculorum. Amen.

Perceptio Corporis tui, Domine Jesu Christe, quod ego indignus sumere præsumo, non mihi proveniat in judicium et condemnationem: sed pro tua pietate prosit mihi ad tutamentum mentis et corporis, et ad medelam percipiendam: Qui vivis et regnas cum Deo Patre in unitate Spiritus Sancti Deus, per omnia sæcula sæculorum. Amen.

Panem cælestem accipiam, et nomen Domini invocabo.

Domine, non sum dignus, ut intres sub tectum meum: sed tantum dic verbo, et sanabitur anima mea. (said three times)

Corpus Domini nostri Jesu Christi custodiat animam meam in vitam æternam. Amen.

Quid retribuam Domino pro omnibus quæ retribuit mihi? Calicem salutaris accipiam, et nomen Domini invocabo. Laudans invocabo Dominum, et ab inimicis meis salvus ero.

Sanguis Domini nostri Jesu Christi custodiat animam meam in vitam æternam. Amen.

life to the world: deliver me by this, Thy most sacred Body and Blood, from all my iniquities and from every evil; make me cling always to Thy commandments, and permit me never to be separated from Thee. Who with the same God, the Father and the Holy Ghost, livest and reignest God, world without end. Amen.

PRAYER FOR GRACE

Let not the partaking of Thy Body, O Lord Jesus Christ, which I, though unworthy, presume to receive, turn to my judgment and condemnation; but through Thy mercy may it be unto me a safeguard and a healing remedy both of soul and body. Who livest and reignest with God the Father, in the unity of the Holy Ghost, God, world without end. Amen.

COMMUNION OF THE PRIEST

I will take the Bread of Heaven, and will call upon the name of the Lord.

Lord, I am not worthy that Thou shouldst enter under my roof; but only say the word, and my soul shall be healed. (said three times)

May the Body of our Lord Jesus Christ preserve my soul unto life everlasting. Amen.

What return shall I make to the Lord for all the things that He hath given unto me? I will take the chalice of salvation, and call upon the Name of the Lord. I will call upon the Lord and give praise: and I shall be saved from mine enemies.

May the Blood of our Lord Jesus Christ preserve my soul unto life everlasting. Amen.

Confiteor (see page 116)

P. Misereatur vestri omnipotens Deus, et dimissis peccatis vestris, perducat vos ad vitam æternam.
S. Amen.
P. Indulgentiam, ✠ absolutionem et remissionem peccatorum vestrorum tribuat vobis omnipotens, et misericors Dominus.
S. Amen.

Ecce Agnus Dei, ecce qui tollit peccata mundi.

Domine, non sum dignus, ut intres sub tectum meum: sed tantum dic verbo, et sanabitur anima mea. (said three times)

Corpus Domini nostri Jesu Christi custodiat animam tuam in vitam æternam. Amen.

Quod ore sumpsimus, Domine, pura mente capiamus: et de munere temporali fiat nobis remedium sempiternum.

Corpus tuum, Domine, quod sumpsi, et Sanguis, quem potavi, adhæreat visceribus meis: et præsta; ut in me non remaneat scelerum macula, quem pura et sancta refecerunt sacramenta: Qui vivis et regnas in sæcula sæculorum. Amen.

P. May Almighty God have mercy on you, forgive you your sins, and bring you to life everlasting.
S. Amen.
P. May the Almighty and Merciful Lord grant you pardon, ✠ absolution, and remission of your sins.
S. Amen.

Behold the Lamb of God, behold Him Who taketh away the sins of the world.

Lord, I am not worthy that Thou shouldst enter under my roof; but only say the word, and my soul shall be healed. (said three times)

May the Body of our Lord Jesus Christ preserve your soul unto life everlasting. Amen.

Prayers after Communion

ABLUTIONS

Grant, O Lord, that what we have taken with our mouth, we may receive with a pure mind; and that from a temporal gift it may become for us an everlasting remedy.

May Thy Body, O Lord, which I have received, and Thy Blood, which I have drunk, cleave to my inmost parts, and grant that no stain of sin remain in me; whom these pure and holy Sacraments have refreshed. Who livest and reignest world without end. Amen.

THE COMMUNION VERSE

Lux æterna luceat eis, Domine: Cum Sanctis tuis in æternum; quia pius es. Requiem æternam dona eis, Domine: et lux perpetua luceat eis. Cum Sanctis tuis in æternum: quia pius es.

P. Dominus vobiscum.
S. Et cum spiritu tuo.
P. Oremus.

THE POSTCOMMUNION

Præsta, quæsumus, omnipotens Deus, ut anima famuli tui (famulæ tuæ) N., quæ hodie de hoc sæculo migravit, his sacrificiis purgata et a peccatis expedita, indulgentiam pariter et requiem capiat sempiternam. Per Dominum nostrum Jesum Christum, Filium tuum, qui tecum vivit et regnat, in unitate Spiritus Sancti, Deus, per omnia sæcula sæculorum.
S. Amen.

P. Dominus vobiscum.
S. Et cum spiritu tuo.

P. Requiescant in pace.
S. Amen.

Placeat tibi, sancta Trinitas, obsequium servitutis meæ: et præsta; ut sacrificium, quod oculis tuæ majestatis indignus obtuli, tibi sit acceptabile, mihique, et omnibus, pro quibus illud obtuli, sit, te miserante, propitiabile. Per Christum Dominum nostrum. Amen.

THE COMMUNION VERSE

May light eternal shine upon them, O Lord: with Thy saints forever, because Thou art merciful. Eternal rest grant unto them, O Lord; and let perpetual light shine upon them. With Thy saints forever, because Thou art merciful.

P. The Lord be with you. **STAND**
S. And with thy spirit. **High Mass**
P. Let us pray.

THE POSTCOMMUNION

Grant, we beseech Thee, almighty God; that the soul of Thy servant (handmaid) N., who this day has departed out of this world, being purified by this sacrifice, and delivered from his (her) sins, may receive both pardon and everlasting rest. Through our Lord Jesus Christ, Thy Son, who liveth and reigneth with Thee in the unity of the Holy Ghost.
S. Amen.

P. The Lord be with you.
S. And with thy spirit.

THE DISMISSAL

P. May they rest in peace.
S. Amen.

May the tribute of my homage be pleasing to Thee, O most holy Trinity. Grant that the Sacrifice which I, unworthy as I am, have offered in the presence of Thy Majesty, may be acceptable to Thee. Through Thy mercy may it bring forgiveness to me and to all for whom I have offered it. Through Christ our Lord. Amen.

THE LAST GOSPEL (see page 49)

THE ABSOLUTION

Non intres in judicium cum servo tuo, Domine, quia nullus apud te justificabitur homo, nisi per te omnium peccatorum ei tribuatur remissio. Non ergo eum, quæsumus, tua judicialis sententia premat, quem tibi vera supplicatio fidei christianæ commendat: sed, gratia tua illi succurrente, mereatur evadere judicium ultionis, qui, dum viveret, insignitus est signaculo sanctæ Trinitatis: Qui vivis et regnas in sæcula sæculorum.

S. Amen.

RESPONSORY: LIBERA ME

Libera me, Domine, de morte æterna, in die illa tremenda: Quando cæli movendi sunt et terra: Dum veneris judicare sæculum per ignem.

Tremens factus sum ego, et timeo, dum discussio venerit, atque ventura ira. Quando cæli movendi sunt et terra.

Dies illa, dies iræ, calamitatis et miseriæ, dies magna et amara valde. Dum veneris judicare sæculum per ignem.

Requiem æternam dona eis, Domine: et lux perpetua luceat eis.

Libera me, Domine, de morte æterna, in die illa tremenda: Quando cæli movendi sunt et terra: Dum veneris judicare sæculum per ignem.

THE ABSOLUTION

STAND

Enter not into judgment with Thy servant, Lord; for in Thy sight no man shall be justified, unless Thou grant him remission of all his sins. We beseech Thee, therefore, that the sentence which Thou pronounce may not fall heavily upon one whom the faithful prayer of Thy Christian people commends to Thee, but rather by the help of Thy grace, may he (she) be found worthy to escape the judgment of condemnation, who in his (her) lifetime was signed with the seal of the Holy Trinity. Thou who livest and reignest for ever and ever. S. Amen.

RESPONSORY: LIBERA ME

Deliver me, Lord, from everlasting death in that awful day: When the heavens and the earth shall be shaken: When Thou shalt come to judge the world by fire.

Dread and trembling have laid hold upon me, and I fear exceedingly because of the judgment and the wrath to come. When the heavens and the earth shall be shaken. When Thou shalt come to judge the world by fire.

O that day, that day of wrath, of sore distress and of all wretchedness, that great and exceedingly bitter day. When Thou shalt come to judge the world by fire.

Eternal rest grant to them, Lord, and let perpetual light shine upon them.

Deliver me, Lord, from everlasting death in that awful day: When the heavens and the earth shall be shaken: When Thou shalt come to judge the world by fire.

P. Kyrie eleison.

S. Christe eleison.

P. Kyrie eleison.

Pater noster ... (inaudibly)

P. Et ne nos inducas in tentationem.

S. Sed libera nos a malo.

P. A porta inferi.

S. Erue, Domine, animam ejus (animas eorum).

P. Requiesca(n)t in pace.

S. Amen.

P. Domine, exaudi orationem meam.

S. Et clamor meus ad te veniat.

P. Dominus vobiscum.

S. Et cum spiritu tuo.

PRAYER

P. Oremus.

Deus, cui proprium est misereri semper et parcere, te supplices exoramus pro anima famuli tui (famulæ tuæ) N., quam hodie de hoc sæculo migrare jussisti: ut non tradas eam in manus inimici, neque obliviscaris in finem, sed iubeas eam a sanctis Angelis suscipi et ad patriam paradisi perduci; ut, quia in te speravit et credidit, non pœnas inferni sustineat, sed gaudia æterna possideat. Per Christum Dominum nostrum.

S. Amen.

P. Lord, have mercy on us.

S. Christ, have mercy on us.

P. Lord, have mercy on us.

Our Father ... (silently)

P. And lead us not into temptation.

S. But deliver us from evil.

P. From the gate of hell.

S. Deliver his (her) soul (their souls), O Lord.

P. May he (she, they) rest in peace.

S. Amen.

P. O Lord, hear my prayer.

S. And let my cry come unto Thee.

P. The Lord be with you.

S. And with your spirit.

PRAYER

P. Let us pray.
O God, whose property it is always to have mercy and to spare, we humbly entreat Thee for the soul of Thy servant N., whom Thou hast summoned today from this world, that Thou wouldst not deliver him (her) into the hands of the enemy, nor forget him (her) for ever, but bid Thy holy Angels receive him (her) and bear him (her) to our home in paradise, so that because he (she) believed and hoped in Thee, he (she) may not undergo the pains of hell but may possess eternal joys. Through Christ our Lord.
S. Amen.

THE BURIAL

ANTIPHON: IN PARADISUM

In paradisum deducant te Angeli: in tuo adventu suscipiant te Martyres, et perducant te in civitatem sanctam Jerusalem. Chorus Angelorum te suscipiat, et cum Lazaro quondam paupere æternam habeas requiem.

BLESSING OF THE GRAVE

Oremus.

Deus, cujus miseratione animæ fidelium requiescunt, hunc tumulum bene✠dicere dignare, eique Angelum tuum sanctum deputa custodem: et quorum quarumque corpora hic sepeliuntur, animas eorum ab omnibus absolve vinculis delictorum; ut in te semper cum Sanctis tuis sine fine lætentur. Per Christum Dominum nostrum.

S. Amen.

Ant. Ego sum resurrectio et vita: qui credit in me, etiam si mortuus fuerit, vivet: et omnis qui vivit, et credit in me non morietur in æternum.

THE BURIAL

ANTIPHON: IN PARADISUM

May the Angels lead you into paradise: may the martyrs receive you at your coming, and lead you into the holy city, Jerusalem. May the choir of Angels receive you, and with Lazarus, who once was poor, may you have everlasting rest.

BLESSING OF THE GRAVE

Let us pray.
O God, by Thy mercy, rest is given to the souls of the faithful; be pleased to bless ✠ this grave. Appoint Thy holy Angels to guard it and set free from all the chains of sin the soul of him (her) whose body is buried here, so that with all Thy saints he (she) may rejoice in Thee forever. Through Christ our Lord.
S. Amen.

Ant. I am the resurrection and the life; he who believes in Me, even if he die, shall live; and whoever lives and believes in Me, shall never die.

CANTICLE LUKE 1:68-69

Benedictus Dominus, Deus Israel, quia visitavit et fecit redemptionem plebis suæ,
Et erexit cornu salutis nobis in domo David pueri sui,
Sicut locutus est per os sanctorum, qui a sæculo sunt, prophetarum ejus:
Salutem ex inimicis nostris, et de manu omnium qui oderunt nos:
Ad faciendam misericordiam cum patribus nostris: memorari testamenti sui sancti:
Jusjurandum, quod juravit ad Abraham, patrem nostrum, daturum se nobis,
Ut sine timore, de manu inimicorum nostrorum liberati, serviamus illi,
In sanctitate et justitia coram ipso omnibus diebus nostris.
Et tu, puer, Propheta Altissimi vocaberis: præibis enim ante faciem Domini parare vias ejus,
Ad dandam scientiam salutis plebi ejus, in remissionem peccatorum eorum
Per viscera misericordiæ Dei nostri, in quibus visitavit nos oriens ex alto,
Illuminare his, qui in tenebris, et in umbra mortis sedent, ad dirigendos pedes nostros in viam pacis.
P. Requiem æternam dona eis, Domine.
S. Et lux perpetua luceat eis.
Ant. Ego sum resurrectio et vita: qui credit in me, etiam si mortuus fuerit, vivet: et omnis qui vivit, et credit in me non morietur in æternum.

P. Kyrie eleison.
S. Christe eleison.
P. Kyrie eleison.
Pater noster ... (inaudibly)

CANTICLE LUKE 1:68-69

Blessed be the Lord, the God of Israel, for He hath visited and wrought the redemption for His people,
And raised up for us a horn of salvation: in the house of David His servant:
As He spoke by the mouth: of His holy prophets of old:
Deliverance from our enemies: and from the hand of all that hate us:
To perform mercy to our fathers: and to remember His holy testament.
The oath which He swore to Abraham our father: that He would grant to us:
That being delivered from the hand of our enemies: we may serve Him without fear,
In holiness and justice before Him: all our days.
And thou, child, shalt be called the prophet of the Most High: for thou shalt go before the Face of the Lord, to prepare His ways:
To give knowledge of salvation to His people: unto remission of their sins:
Through the tender mercy of our God: in which the Day-spring from on high hath visited us:
To enlighten those who sit in darkness, and in the shadow of death: to direct our feet into the way of peace.
P. Eternal rest grant unto them, O Lord.
S. And let perpetual light shine upon them.
Ant. I am the resurrection and the life; he who believes in Me, even if he die, shall live; and whoever lives and believes in Me, shall never die.

P. Lord, have mercy on us.
S. Christ, have mercy on us.
P. Lord, have mercy on us.
Our Father … (silently)

P. Et ne nos inducas in tentationem.

S. Sed libera nos a malo.

P. A porta inferi.

S. Erue, Domine, animam ejus (animas eorum).

P. Requiesca(n)t in pace.

S. Amen.

P. Domine, exaudi orationem meam.

S. Et clamor meus ad te veniat.

P. Dominus vobiscum.

S. Et cum spiritu tuo.

P. Oremus.
Fac, quæsumus, Domine, hanc cum servo tuo defuncto (ancilla tua defuncta) misericordiam, ut factorum suorum in pœnis non recipiat vicem, qui (quæ) tuam in votis tenuit voluntatem: ut, sicut hic eum (eam) vera fides junxit fidelium turmis; ita illic eum (eam) tua miseratio societ angelicis choris. Per Christum Dominum nostrum.
S. Amen.

P. Requiem æternam dona ei, Domine.
S. Et lux perpetua luceat ei.
P. Requiescat in pace.
S. Amen.
P. Anima ejus, et animæ omnium fidelium defunctorum per misericordiam Dei requiescant in pace.
S. Amen.

P. And lead us not into temptation.

S. But deliver us from evil.

P. From the gate of hell.

S. Deliver his (her) soul (their souls), O Lord.

P. May he (she, they) rest in peace.

S. Amen.

P. O Lord, hear my prayer.

S. And let my cry come unto Thee.

P. The Lord be with you.

S. And with your spirit.

P. Let us pray.
Lord, we implore Thee, grant this mercy to Thy departed servant that he (she) who held fast to Thy will in intention, may not receive punishment in return for his (her) deeds; so that, as the true faith united him (her) with the body of the faithful on earth; Thy mercy may unite him (her) with the company of the choirs of Angels in heaven. Through Christ our Lord.
S. Amen.

P. Eternal rest grant unto him (her), O Lord.
S. And let perpetual light shine upon him (her).
P. May he (she) rest in peace.
S. Amen.
P. May his (her) soul, and the souls of all the faithful departed, through the mercy of God rest in peace.
S. Amen.

Christ in Majesty
Fra Angelico

The Rite of Baptism

1962 Typical Edition

Baptism of Christ
Fra Angelico

ORDO BAPTISMI UNIUS PARVULI

(Rit. Rom., Tit. II, Cap. II)

Ad limen ecclesiæ

Sacerdos interrogat infantem:

N. Quid petis ab Ecclesia Dei?	N., what do you ask of the Church of God?

Patrinus respondet:

Fidem.	The faith.

Sacerdos:

Fides, quid tibi præstat?	What does the faith offer you?

Patrinus respondet:

Vitam æternam.	Eternal life.

2. Sacerdos:

Si igitur vis ad vitam ingredi, serva mandata. Diliges Dominum Deum tuum ex toto corde tuo, et ex tota anima tua, et ex tota mente tua, et proximum tuum sicut teipsum.	If, then, you wish to enter into life, keep the commandments: you shall love the Lord your God with your whole heart, and with your whole soul, and with your whole mind, and your neighbor as yourself.

3. Deinde ter exsufflat leniter in faciem infantis, et dicit semel:

Exi ab eo (ea), immunde spiritus, et da locum Spiritui Sancto Paraclito.	Depart from him (her), unclean spirit, and give place to the Holy Spirit, the Consoler.

4. Postea pollice facit signum crucis in fronte et in pectore infantis, dicens:

Accipe signum Crucis tam in fron✠te, quam in cor✠de, sume fidem cælestium præceptorum: et talis esto moribus, ut templum Dei jam esse possis.

Receive the mark of the cross on your ✠ forehead and within your ✠ heart. Embrace the faith with its divine teachings. So live that you will indeed be a temple of God.

Oratio

Oremus.

Preces nostras, quæsumus, Domine, clementer exaudi: et hunc electum tuum N. (hanc electam tuam N.) crucis Dominicæ impressione signatum(-am) perpetua virtute custodi: ut, magnitudinis gloriæ tuæ rudimenta servans, per custodiam mandatorum tuorum ad regenerationis gloriam pervenire mereatur. Per Christum Dominum nostrum.

R. Amen.

Let us pray.

We beg Thee, Lord God, graciously hear our prayers. Guard Thy chosen one, N., with the never-failing power of the cross of Christ, with which he (she) has been marked. Protect him (her) so that, remaining true to the first lessons he (she) has learned about the great glory Thou wilt confer upon him (her), he (she) may, by keeping Thy commandments, attain to the glory of a new birth. Through Christ our Lord.

R. Amen.

5. Deinde imponit manum super caput infantis, et postea, manum extensam tenens, dicit:

Oratio

Oremus.

Omnipotens, sempiterne Deus, Pater Domini nostri Jesu Christi, respicere dignare super hunc famulum tuum N. (hanc famulam tuam N.) quem (quam) ad rudimenta fidei vocare dignatus es; omnem cæcitatem cordis ab eo (ea) expelle; disrumpe omnes laqueos satanæ, quibus fuerat colligatus(-a); aperi ei, Domine, januam pietatis tuæ, ut, signo sapientiæ tuæ imbutus(-a), omnium cupiditatum fœtoribus careat, et ad suavem odorem præceptorum tuorum lætus(-a) tibi in Ecclesia tua deserviat et proficiat de die in diem. Per eumdem Christum Dominum nostrum.

R. Amen.

Let us pray.

Almighty and eternal God, Father of our Lord Jesus Christ, look with favor upon this Thy servant, N., whom Thou hast called to take his (her) first steps in the faith. Take from him (her) all blindness of heart. Free him (her) from the snares of Satan which until now have held him (her). Open to him (her), Lord, the gate of Thy mercy. Then, seasoned by the salt which is symbolic of Thy wisdom, may he (she) be relieved of the corruption of evil desires; and, finding pleasure in the keeping of Thy commandments, may he (she) serve Thee in Thy Church and make progress from day to day in the way of perfection. Through the same Christ our Lord.

R. Amen.

6. Deinde sacerdos benedicit sal, quod semel benedictum alias ad eumdem usum deservire potest.

Benedictio salis

Exorcizo te, creatura salis, in nomine Dei ✠ Patris omnipotentis, et in caritate Domini nostri Jesu ✠ Christi, et in virtute Spiritus ✠ Sancti. Exorcizo te per Deum ✠ vivum, per Deum ✠ verum, per Deum ✠ sanctum, per Deum ✠ qui te ad tutelam humani generis procreavit, et populo venienti ad credulitatem per servos suos consecrari præcepit, ut in nomine sanctæ Trinitatis efficiaris salutare sacramentum ad effugandum inimicum, Proinde rogamus te, Domine Deus noster, ut hanc creaturam salis sanctificando sancti✠fices, et benedicendo bene✠dicas, ut fiat omnibus accipientibus perfecta medicina, permanens in visceribus eorum, in nomine ejusdem Domini nostri Jesu Christi, qui venturus est judicare vivos et mortuos, et sæculum per ignem.

R. Amen.

7. Deinde immittit modicum salis benedicti in os infantis, dicens:

N. Accipe sal sapientiæ: propitiatio sit tibi in vitam æternam.

R. Amen.

N., receive the salt, which is a symbol of wisdom. May it bring you God's favor for life everlasting.

R. Amen.

Sacerdos

Pax tecum.

R. Et cum spiritu tuo.

Peace be with you.

R. And with thy spirit.

Oratio

Oremus.

Deus patrum nostrorum, Deus universæ conditor veritatis, te supplices exoramus, ut hunc famulum tuum N. (hanc famulam tuam N.) respicere digneris propitius, et hoc primum pabulum salis gustantem, non diutius esurire permittas, quo minus cibo expleatur cælesti, quatenus sit semper spiritu fervens, spe gaudens, tuo semper nomini serviens. Perduc eum (eam), Domine, quæsumus, ad novæ regenerationis lavacrum, ut cum fidelibus tuis promissionum tuarum æterna præmia consequi mereatur. Per Christum Dominum nostrum.

R. Amen.

Let us pray.

God of our fathers, God, the Author of all truth, we humbly ask Thee to look with favor on this Thy servant, N., who has had his (her) first taste of blessed food in the form of salt. Satisfy him (her) with the bread of heaven, so that he (she) may be forever fervent in spirit, joyful in hope, and zealous in Thy service. We ask Thee, Lord, to lead him (her) to the waters in which he (she) will be born again, so that he (she), with all who believe in Thee, may obtain the unending rewards which Thou hast promised. Through Christ our Lord.

R. Amen.

Exorcizo te, immunde spiritus, in nomine Pa✠tris, et Fi✠lii, et Spiritus ✠ Sancti, ut exeas, et recedas ab hoc famulo (hac famula) Dei N.: Ipse enim tibi imperat, maledicte damnate, qui pedibus super mare ambulavit, et Petro mergenti dexteram porrexit.

Ergo, maledicte diabole, recognosce sententiam tuam, et da honorem Deo vivo et vero, da honorem Jesu Christo Filio ejus, et Spiritui Sancto, et recede ab hoc famulo (hac famula) Dei N., quia istum (istam) sibi Deus, et Dominus noster Jesus Christus ad suam sanctam gratiam, et benedictionem, fontemque Baptismatis vocare dignatus est.

8. Hic pollice in fronte signat infantem, dicens:

Et hoc signum sanctæ Cru✠cis, quod nos fronti ejus damus, tu, maledicte diabole, numquam audeas violare. Per eumdem Christum Dominum nostrum.

R. Amen.

Accursed devil, never dare to desecrate this sign of the holy ✠ cross which we are tracing upon his (her) forehead. Through the same Christ our Lord.

R. Amen.

9. Mox imponit manum super caput infantis, et postea, manum extensam tenens, dicit:

Oratio

Oremus.

Æternam, ac justissimam pietatem tuam deprecor, Domine sancte, Pater omnipotens, æterne Deus, auctor luminis et veritatis, super hunc famulum tuum N. (hanc famulam tuam N.) ut digneris eum (eam) illuminare lumine intelligentiæ tuæ: munda eum (eam) et sanctifica: da ei scientiam veram, ut dignus(-a) gratia Bap-

Let us pray.

Lord, holy Father, almighty and eternal God, source of all light and truth, I humbly beg Thy never-ending and most holy mercy upon this servant of Thine, N. May it please Thee to grant him (her) the light of Thine own wisdom. Cleanse him (her) and make him (her) holy. Give him (her) true knowledge, so that he (she) may

tismi tui effectus(-a), teneat firmam spem, consilium rectum, doctrinam sanctam. Per Christum Dominum nostrum.

R. Amen.

be made worthy of the grace of Thy Baptism and may maintain firm hope, sound judgment, and a grasp of holy doctrine.Through Christ our Lord.

R. Amen.

In ecclesia

10. Postea sacerdos imponit extremam partem stolæ pendentem a suo humero sinistro super infantem, et introducit eum in ecclesiam, dicens:

N. Ingredere in templum Dei, ut habeas partem cum Christo in vitam æternam.

R. Amen.

N., enter into the temple of God, so that you may have part with Christ in everlasting life.

R. Amen.

11. Cum fuerint ecclesiam ingressi, sacerdos procedens ad fontem, cum susceptoribus conjunctim clara voce dicit:

Credo in Deum, Patrem omnipotentem, Creatorem cæli et terræ. Et in Jesum Christum, Filium ejus unicum, Dominum nostrum: qui conceptus est de Spiritu Sancto, natus ex Maria Virgine, passus sub Pontio Pilato, crucifixus, mortuus, et sepultus: descendit ad inferos; tertia die resurrexit a mortuis; ascendit ad cælos; sedet ad dexteram Dei Patris omnipotentis: inde venturus est judi-

I believe in God, the Father almighty, Creator of heaven and earth; and in Jesus Christ, His only Son, our Lord, who was conceived by the Holy Ghost, born of the Virgin Mary, suffered under Pontius Pilate, was crucified, died, and was buried. He descended into hell; the third day He arose again from the dead; He ascended into heaven, sitteth at the right hand of God, the Father

care vivos et mortuos. Credo in Spiritum Sanctum, sanctam Ecclesiam catholicam, Sanctorum communionem, remissionem peccatorum, carnis resurrectionem, vitam æternam. Amen.

almighty; thence He shall come to judge the living and the dead. I believe in the Holy Ghost, the holy Catholic Church, the communion of saints, the forgiveness of sins, the resurrection of the body, and life everlasting. Amen.

Pater noster, qui es in cælis, sanctificetur nomen tuum. Adveniat regnum tuum. Fiat voluntas tua, sicut in cælo, et in terra. Panem nostrum quotidianum da nobis hodie. Et dimitte nobis debita nostra, sicut et nos dimittimus debitoribus nostris. Et ne nos inducas in tentationem: sed libera nos a malo. Amen.

Our Father, who art in heaven, hallowed be Thy name; Thy kingdom come; Thy will be done on earth as it is in heaven. Give us this day our daily bread; and forgive us our trespasses as we forgive those who trespass against us; and lead us not into temptation, but deliver us from evil. Amen.

12. Ac deinde, antequam accedat ad baptisterium, versis renibus ostio cancellorum baptisterii, dicit:

Exorcismus

Exorcizo te, omnis spiritus immunde in nomine Dei ✠ Patris omnipotentis, et in nomine Jesu ✠ Christi Filii ejus, Domini et Judicis nostri, et in virtute Spiritus ✠ Sancti, ut discedas ab hoc plasmate Dei N., quod Dominus noster ad templum sanctum suum vocare dignatus est, ut fiat templum Dei vivi, et Spiritus Sanctus habitet in eo. Per eumdem Chris-

tum Dominum nostrum, qui venturus est judicare vivos et mortuos, et sæculum per ignem.

R. Amen.

13. Postea sacerdos pollice accipit de saliva oris sui (quod omittitur quotiescumque rationabilis adest causa munditiei tuendæ aut periculum morbi contrahendi vel propagandi quin tamen in tali casu tactus præscriptus cum sua formula omittatur); et tangit aures et nares infantis: tangendo vero aurem dexteram et sinistram dicit:

Ephpheta, quod est, Adaperire.

Deinde tangit nares, dicens:

In odorem suavitatis. Tu autem effugare, diabole; appropinquabit enim judicium Dei.

14. Postea interrogat baptizandum nominatim, dicens:

N. Abrenuntias satanæ?	N., do you renounce Satan?

Respondet patrinus:

Abrenuntio.	I do renounce him.

Sacerdos:

Et omnibus operibus ejus?	And all his works?

Patrinus:

Abrenuntio.	I do renounce them.

Sacerdos:

Et omnibus pompis ejus?	And all his allurements?

Patrinus:

Abrenuntio.	I do renounce them.

Unctio olei

15. Deinde sacerdos intingit pollicem in oleo catechumenorum, et infantem ungit in pectore, et inter scapulas in modum crucis, dicens semel:

Ego te linio ✠ oleo salutis in Christo Jesu Domino nostro, ut habeas vitam æternam.

R. Amen.

16. Subinde pollicem et inuncta loca abstergit bombacio, vel re simili.

In baptisterio

17. Stans ibidem extra cancellos, deponit stolam violaceam, et sumit stolam albi coloris. Tunc ingreditur baptisterium, in quod intrat etiam patrinus cum infante.

Sacerdos ad fontem interrogat, expresso nomine, baptizandum, patrino respondente:

N. Credis in Deum Patrem omnipotentem, Creatorem cæli et terræ?

R. Credo.

Credis in Jesum Christum, Filium ejus unicum, Dominum nostrum, natum, et passum?

R. Credo.

Credis et in Spiritum Sanctum, sanctam Ecclesiam catholicam, Sanctorum communionem, remissionem peccatorum, carnis resurrectionem, et vitam æternam?

R. Credo.

N., do you believe in God, the Father almighty, Creator of heaven and earth?

R. I do believe.

Do you believe in Jesus Christ, His only Son, our Lord, Who was born into this world and Who suffered?

R. I do believe.

Do you believe also in the Holy Spirit, the holy Catholic Church, the communion of saints, the forgiveness of sins, the resurrection of the body, and life everlasting?

R. I do believe.

18. Subinde, expresso nomine baptizandi, sacerdos dicit:

N. Vis baptizari?	N., do you wish to be baptized?

Respondet patrinus:

Volo.	I do.

Baptismus

19. Tunc patrino, vel matrina, vel utroque (si ambo admittantur) infantem tenente, sacerdos vasculo seu urceolo accipit aquam baptismalem, et eam ter fundit super caput infantis in modum crucis, et simul verba proferens, semel tantum distincte et attende, dicit:

N. Ego te baptizo in nomine Pa✠tris, (fundit primo), et Fi✠lii, (fundit secundo), et Spiritus ✠ Sancti, (fundit tertio).

20. Ubi autem est consuetudo baptizandi per immersionem, sacerdos accipit infantem, et, advertens ne lædatur, caute immergit, et trina immersione baptizat, et semel tantum dicit:

N. Ego te baptizo in nomine Pa✠tris, et Fi✠lii, et Spiritus ✠ Sancti.

21. Mox patrinus, vel matrina, vel uterque simul infantem de sacro fonte levant, suscipientes illum de manu sacerdotis.

22. Si vero dubitetur, an infans fuerit baptizatus, utatur hac forma:

N. Si non es baptizatus (a), ego te baptizo in nomine Pa✠tris, et Fi✠lii, et Spiritus ✠ Sancti.

Unctio chrismatis, etc.

23. Deinde intingit pollicem in sacro chrismate, et ungit infantem in summitate capitis in modum crucis, dicens:

Deus omnipotens, Pater Domini nostri Jesu Christi, qui te regeneravit ex aqua et Spiritu Sancto, quique dedit tibi remissionem omnium peccatorum (hic inungit), ipse te liniat ✠ Chrismate salutis in eodem Christo Jesu Domino nostro in vitam æternam. R. Amen.

Sacerdos:

Pax tibi.
R. Et cum spiritu tuo.

Peace be with you.
R. And with thy spirit.

24. Tum bombacio, vel re simili, abstergit pollicem et locum inunctum, et imponit capiti ejus linteolum candidum loco vestis albæ, dicens:

Accipe vestem candidam, quam perferas immaculatam ante tribunal Domini nostri Jesu Christi, ut habeas vitam æternam.

R. Amen.

Receive this white garment. Never let it become stained, so that, when you stand before the judgment seat of our Lord Jesus Christ, you may have life everlasting.

R. Amen.

25. Postea dat ei, vel patrino, candelam accensam, dicens:

Accipe lampadem ardentem, et irreprehensibilis custodi Baptismum tuum: serva Dei mandata, ut, cum Dominus venerit ad nuptias, possis occurrere ei una cum omnibus Sanctis in aula cælesti, et vivas in sæcula sæculorum.

R. Amen.

Receive this burning light, and keep the grace of your baptism throughout a blameless life. Observe the commandments of God. Then, when the Lord comes to the heavenly wedding feast, you will be able to meet him with all the saints in the halls of heaven, and live forever and ever.

R. Amen.

26. Postremo dicit:

N. Vade in pace, et Dominus sit tecum.

R. Amen.

N., go in peace, and the Lord be with you.

R. Amen.